# Housing

SOCIAL
SERVICE
SERIES
No. 1

HOUSING.

SOCIAL SERVICE HANDBOOKS
No. I

# HOUSING

BY

## PERCY ALDEN, M.P.

*Author of " The Unemployed "*

AND

## EDWARD E. HAYWARD, M.A.

*Hon. Adviser on Housing to British Institute of Social Service*

*SECOND EDITION.*

𝔏𝔬𝔫𝔡𝔬𝔫:

HEADLEY BROTHERS
BISHOPSGATE STREET WITHOUT, E.C.

FIRST EDITION, MARCH, 1907.
SECOND EDITION, APRIL, 1907.

ALL RIGHTS RESERVED.

# PREFATORY NOTE.

THIS little handbook does not profess to be anything more than an introduction to the study of the problem of Housing. It is one of a series, the object of which is to assist Social Service Committees and organizations of working men who are striving to promote, by voluntary effort, the public health and well-being of the towns in which they live.

It was felt that the study of any one social problem too often necessitated the purchase of costly books, and the attempt is therefore made to bring together in a compact and cheap form all the important facts that bear on the subject.

For more detailed information students should consult Mr. W. Thompson's "Housing Handbook" and the supplement recently issued. The writers, and indeed all social reformers, are under a deep obligation to him for the mass of valuable statistics which his book contains.

We desire to acknowledge the kindness of the British Institute of Social Service in compiling for us the little Bibliography which we have appended, and for the assistance in several directions it has readily granted.

PERCY ALDEN,

EDWARD E. HAYWARD.

# CONTENTS.

# HOUSING.

## CHAPTER I.

### INTRODUCTION.—THE PROBLEM STATED.

"I am certain that I speak the truth, and a truth which can be confirmed by all experienced persons—clergy, medical men, and all who are conversant with the working class—that until their housing conditions are Christianised, all hope of moral or social improvement is utterly in vain." (LORD SHAFTESBURY.)

THE Housing Problem, which has reached such an acute stage in most civilised countries to-day, is by no means a new problem; the need for its solution has, however, received additional emphasis by reason of the immense increase in our urban population due to the industrial revolution. It has become a truism to say that unhealthy houses and insanitary surroundings are unfavourable to the growth of healthy and virtuous citizens, but it is only of late years that this fact has been borne in upon the nation as a whole. The result has been a great awakening of the interest displayed in this important question, an interest which is manifest in the better administration of existing legislative enactments on the part of local authorities.

In its present form the housing problem began to be urgent about the middle of last century, when the factory system was working out its significant change in the conditions of Great Britain. The marked exodus from country to town, a movement which as yet shows no signs of abatement, brought the whole question of housing into prominence, and compelled the attention both of municipalities and the legislature; a long and bitter struggle for reform at last resulted in the appointment in 1884 of the Royal Commission on Housing. This was one outcome of that strenuous feeling on social matters, which was a characteristic mark of the whole country in the "eighties." All sections of the community began to realise that there had arisen, as an indirect result of the very prosperity which a period of industrial invention had created, a housing problem of the first importance and of the greatest complexity. Encouraged by Royalty and strengthened by reformers of all parties, the Housing Commission attacked almost for the first time the problem of the town, with its overcrowded tenements, its squalid rookeries, and its insanitary slums.

**1.—The Town Problem.** The problem which presented itself was briefly as follows:— The country had been passing through a period of unprecedented prosperity and commercial activity, due to the introduction of machinery and the growth of the factory system. The towns and cities, acting as a sort of gigantic magnet, attracted to themselves hordes of country labourers who were feeling at this time the depression in agriculture. The population of these urban areas grew with such rapidity that the municipalities, untaught by experience and lacking men of ideas and foresight, found themselves unable to cope with this inrush of new life or to create the necessary machinery for dealing with it. No scientific or well-planned effort was made to supply effective housing accommodation, and as a consequence large masses of the working classes, compelled to live near the factory owing to the exigencies of their labour, were crowded into unhealthy and insanitary slums; while the worst forms of jerry-building were pardoned or condoned on the ground that the insistent demand for more houses must be satisfied. The Housing Reformer, then, found himself face to face with a problem rendered complicated and difficult by reason of the constant reaction of other social evils which resulted from the same cause, and thus it is that a solution of the housing problem would enable us to attack with more confidence the pauperism and crime, the drunkenness, physical degeneration and high death rate of our great cities.

2.—The Problem of Overcrowding. The question as to whether there is a sufficiency or insufficiency of housing accommodation depends mainly on our definition of overcrowding. "We may be tolerably certain," say the Census Commissioners of 1891, "that the rooms in tenements with less than five rooms will not in any but exceptional cases be of large size, and that ordinary tenements which have more than two occupants per room, bedrooms and sitting-rooms included, may safely be considered as unduly overcrowded." According to this definition there were, in 1901, 392,414 overcrowded tenements in which were living 2,667,506 persons. Thus 8.2 per cent. of the whole population of England and Wales was returned officially as overcrowded in the last census. This is a desirable decrease on the census of 1891, where 481,653 tenements were overcrowded, in which were living 3,258,044 persons, or 11.2 per cent. of the total population; which justifies the Commissioners in 1901 in remarking, "However the tenement figures are compared, it is impossible to avoid the conclusion that the comparison affords satisfactory evidence of distinct improvement in the housing of the people during the ten years 1891-1901."* We are also told that 3,186,640 persons occupy three-room tenements, and 2,158,644 two-room tenements; whilst not less than 507,763 live in dwellings of only one room in England to-day.

---

* Census Commissioners of 1901, pp. 40, 42.

Often in this one room these people have to rear their children, eat, sleep, dress, cook, live and possibly die, unless they are among those who breathe their last in the more spacious infirmary or prison, To-day in London, with all its immense wealth, two-thirds of the whole population live in dwellings of not more than four rooms in all. In such cities as Glasgow, Edinburgh, Liverpool, Dublin and even Birmingham, conditions are quite as bad, if not worse. In Glasgow, where municipal enterprise has made such splendid progress, "no less than one-fifth of the people live in one-room dwellings, and more than half the people have houses of not more than two rooms. In Edinburgh, 'the Modern Athens,' more than half the houses consist of one and two rooms. while in some districts, such as Canongate and St. Giles', the proportion is as high as seventy per cent. In Newcastle, Gateshead, Sunderland, and the counties of Northumberland and Durham, one-third of the total population, urban and rural, live in overcrowded houses."*

3.—**A Minimum Standard.** What then is the standard aimed at by the majority of housing reformers? What is the least accommodation necessary for decently, healthily and comfortably housing the mass of the working people of this country? We know that it is unwise to put this standard too high, for by making unnecessarily stringent conditions, we are apt to increase the

* "Housing Handbook," p. 4. W. Thompson.

difficulties of those who have a practical concern in this matter, and have to administer the law as members of our public authorities.

The minimum for the average working man's family is a cheap, but well-built house with four or five suitable rooms, together with a quarter-acre garden, or at least with a fair-sized court-yard. The site should be a healthy one and the house perfectly sanitary, well-lighted, well-ventilated and well-drained. And this accommodation must be supplied at a low rental, or it will be found beyond the means of the working classes. All who have any knowledge of the subject say that such accommodation is seldom or never found either in town or country. The first difficulty is a financial one. A sufficiently high standard of dwelling is not provided for the masses of our people, because they cannot afford to pay the necessary rent. The wages of the unskilled labourer are for the most part subsistence wages, and do not admit of paying the high rents which are charged in our big cities for even the poorest accommodation. It is probably true that in some cases overcrowding is due to carelessness and failure to use to the best advantage existing accommodation, but this will not go far to explain the miserable conditions we have described.

4.—**The House Famine.** The most important factor in the whole Housing problem is the serious house famine which exists generally in this country. The dearth of houses will explain

one cause at least of the high rents as well as the overcrowding. The statistics as to deficient accommodation are conclusive, and this notwithstanding the fact that an enormous number of insanitary houses are still occupied and will probably be occupied for years to come. "We find in the first place, that if every room, good and bad, occupied or unoccupied, in all the workmen's dwellings in the country be reckoned as existing accommodation, there are not enough of any sort to house the working population without unhealthy overcrowding; and if only healthy rooms are reckoned, the position is infinitely worse. In the second place, we find that so far from new rooms being built in sufficient quantities to make up the deficiency, there is a distinct lessening of the rate of increase, and (so far as healthy dwellings are concerned) no prospect of relieving the intensity of the 'famine' to any appreciable extent." *

Nor is this condition of affairs confined to our cities. The same writer states that "even in the rural districts, where population is either stationary or diminishing, the supply has been unequal to the demand." In 1897 an investigation was made into housing conditions in nearly 400 villages in various parts of England on behalf of the Land Law Reform Association; this revealed the fact that in half the villages, the cottages were "unsatisfactory" or "very bad," and that "in over a quarter there were not enough houses for the people."

* "Housing Handbook," pp. 1 and 2.

We shall have occasion to mention this scarcity in house accommodation more than once again. It lies at the root of the whole Housing question. It is not enough to improve existing property, we must increase the supply of houses. " Fundamentally the problem resolves itself into an increase of the effective supply of houses. In the inner ring of London this is the one political problem which directly affects the life of the people." *

5.—**Failure of Private Enterprise.** How can we account for this state of affairs ? The first and most obvious reply is that private enterprise has failed to keep pace with the demand. It has so failed for many reasons, but chiefly because the whole concern of providing housing accommodation for the poorer classes does not give a sufficiently large return on the money invested. In justice to the good builder it must be said that, now building materials are so much more expensive, it is practically impossible to build houses at cheap rents and at the same time not infringe the local bye-laws. "It cannot be too strongly insisted upon that the increased cost of building has more to do with the house famine in suburban and rural districts than the cost of land." † The latter fact has, however, as we shall see, an important bearing on the problem. Whatever the cause, the ill effects of this serious scarcity of dwell-

---

* " Towards a Social Policy " (The *Speaker*), chap. x.
† " Housing Handbook," p. 10.

ings are the same. Families which under normal conditions would be living in two or three rooms, have to be content with one, and that all too small for the varied needs of its inmates. Workers, who should rightly be occupying a four-roomed house or cottage-flat, have to live in a two or three-roomed tenement; and so on right up the scale, for the house famine affects the whole mass of the working-classes, even the well-to-do artisans. To the poorest of the poor, it simply means that no accommodation is forthcoming at all except in the worst slums. "When we read of families seeking admission to our workhouses owing to their inability to secure accommodation, we certainly get a glimpse of the house famine in our midst, and it requires but a slight intercourse with the people themselves in order to appreciate the unparalleled scarcity of house accommodation."*

Scarcity of supply in a case like this is bound to mean monopoly value, and high rents are the result. We find an average rent of 7s. 6d. per week for three rooms in suburban London, while as much as 6s. 6d. a week can be got for one room in Central London, which means a yearly rental of over £16 per room. Dr. Bowmaker rightly observes, "Until we have relieved the tension and dealt with the deficiency of the supply, we can do nothing to check the upward tendency of rents or cope with the evil of overcrowding. So long as the present conditions exist, so long as

---

* Fabian Tract, No. 101. Part III. Edward Bowmaker, M.D.

B

a single room, nay, even a part of a room, possesses such an artificial value, so long must our efforts be foredoomed to failure."

We will mention only one other evil effect of this scarcity of house accommodation. Many of the houses for which these exorbitant rents are asked are thoroughly insanitary and consequently dangerous, both to the inhabitants and the community at large. The useful sanitary legislation which already exists cannot, in many cases, be put into operation for the simple reason that a strict enforcement of the law would make large numbers of men and women absolutely homeless. In fact, until we have more houses for our working people, any further reform in the way of removal of insanitary dwellings is extremely difficult, inflicting as it does real hardship upon those who can least afford to suffer.

7.—Summary of Problem. The Housing Problem then may be practically summed up as follows :—We must regard four things as absolutely essential if men, women and children are to live healthily and decently in our great cities.

1. Too many people must not live in any one room or house.
2. Too many houses must not be built on any given area of land.
3. The houses must be well-built, well-lighted, well-ventilated, and well-drained.
4. There must be a sufficient number of houses for the whole population.

Bearing these points in mind it is necessary to show how far short we have fallen of this ideal both in country and town, and then to state not only the attempts to remedy the evil which are in operation to-day, but those more drastic and sweeping measures which have been suggested by reformers and legislators.

# CHAPTER II.

HISTORICAL RETROSPECT—EXISTING LEGISLATION.

----

"A solution of the great difficulties connected with the housing question can be expected only from the long continued co-operation of the economic and social influences of the community, with the legislative and administrative powers of the state" (PRUSSIAN DECREE ON HOUSING, 1901).

----

IT is, of course, only of recent years that the community has deliberately pledged itself to the work of seeing that the citizens are properly housed. But for many centuries the old boroughs and corporations of England have had the management and ownership of houses and buildings. There are still towns and cities that draw a considerable portion of their income from the rents of such property. Even so far back as the fourteenth century, the power to hold land and to own the buildings upon it was vested in the municipality. It has been pointed out that in the reign of Henry VIII. powers were given to the municipal authorities to rebuild the house property in the towns which had fallen into disrepair and confusion owing to the wars of succession, and such property in a considerable number of cases eventually fell into the hands of the local authorities. It is fairly certain that in the eighteenth century one function of the local government was to rebuild houses and premises destroyed by fire, and this seems to suggest that fire insurance was also at that time a municipal function. In the last century the growing feeling in favour of better housing makes its appearance even in the writings of our poets and essayists. Wordsworth refers to the poor as—

"Barricaded evermore
Within the walls of cities;"

and Carlyle was sufficiently scathing in his condemnation of those who shut out from the working classes the right to life and to light. It was Lord Shaftesbury, however, who, as a social reformer, approached the question of housing from a practical standpoint. The Labourers' Friend Society, afterwards the Society for Improving the Condition of the Labouring Classes, was largely the result of his agitation in 1842. It aimed at creating a standard of housing for the working classes, and the society contended that " the moral were almost equal to the physical benefits, and that although numbers would refuse or abuse the boon extended to them, many would accept it joyfully and turn it to good account." Of this Society the Prince Consort became President. In 1851 Lord Shaftesbury introduced a Bill to "encourage the establishment of lodging-houses for the working classes." For various reasons the Act was almost a dead letter. It was not until thirty-four years later that the first real Housing Act was passed. We must not, however, forget the indirect effect of the Public Health Act of 1875. We may say that at this date, *i.e.* at the beginning of the last quarter of the nineteenth century—commences any effective legislation for the better housing of the people.

1.—The Public Health Acts. It is true that we previously had The Nuisances Act and The Prevention of Diseases Act (1855), but these were but tentative measures which were made sure in the Public Health Act of 1875. This Act was especially supplemented for London by the Public Health (London) Acts of 1891 and 1902, and for Scotland by the Public Health (Scotland) Act of 1897. By these Acts, as is well known, all Borough Councils (and in default of any one of these the County Council of that county in which the borough is situated) are appointed the proper sanitary authorities to enquire into all matters of the public health.

Chief Clauses. It is the duty of these authorities:—(1) To adopt such Bye-laws as the Act provides, so as to secure the construction, draining and cleansing of streets, removal of house refuse, proper building of houses, etc., *e.g.* there must be good foundations, party walls of regulation thickness, a damp course, incombustible roof, properly built chimneys, rain-water gutters, proper sanitary conveniences and sufficient water supply (in the case of London for *all* houses, in the case of England and Wales for new houses or houses rebuilt). Underground dwellings are only permitted under specially stringent conditions. Where these housing conditions are not fulfilled, the sanitary authority, after giving due notice, may issue an order declaring the building to be "unfit for human habitation" and, unless repaired, may close it by a similar order.

(2) To receive the compulsory notification of all cases of infectious disease and to carefully enquire into and remove any "*nuisance.*" A nuisance is defined (1891) as (*a*) any premises or part of premises in such a condition as to be a "nuisance or injurious to health"; (*b*) any animal or deposit of material so kept as to be a "nuisance or injury to health"; (*c*) any house or part of a house so overcrowded as to be *dangerous or injurious to the health* of the inhabitants; (*d*) any chimney other than that of a private house emitting such quantities of smoke as to be a nuisance.

(3) To carry out such inspection (especially in the case of Common Lodging Houses), both Sanitary and Medical, as shall ensure the bye-laws being fulfilled and the nuisances prevented.

2.—The Royal Commission of 1884. The next event of importance for housing reformers was the Royal Commission, appointed March 4th, 1884, "to enquire into the Housing of the Working Classes in the United Kingdom." Upon this commission sat our present King, who shewed an appreciative and sympathetic interest in all the proceedings, Cardinal Manning, Lord Salisbury, Sir Charles Dilke (chairman), and many other influential persons. The Report of the Commissioners appeared (1885) in two large volumes and contains almost all the recommendations which housing reformers, then and since, have urged upon Parliament. It is needless here to go into the details of these suggested reforms, as we shall have to discuss them when we come to deal with the question of remedies. Unfortunately, the legislative result was in no way equal to the ability and earnestness of those who worked on this Commission ; but much was brought to light, especially in the sympathetic evidence of the Earl of Shaftesbury, which it has been highly advantageous for the country to hear and to discuss.

3.—The Housing Act (1890). It is when we come to the Housing of the Working Classes Act of 1890, with the amending Acts of 1900 and 1903, that we find the chief legislative measures for housing reform ; and doubtless the main Act was, in no small degree, due to the Commission we have just mentioned. It contained not much that was new, and far less than the Commissioners had recommended ; it was rather a consolidating Act, collecting and revising such measures as had been adopted in Torrens's Act of 1868 (amended in 1879 and 1882), and Cross's Act of 1875 (amended also in 1879 and 1882). The Act consists of seven parts, three only of which we need describe in any detail.

**Part I.** Part I., which applies to the London County Council and all Urban District Councils and Towns Councils, provides for the clearance, by the sanitary authority in question, of large *unhealthy areas*. An area is said to be unhealthy if it contain (*a*) "any houses, courts, or alleys . . . unfit for human habitation," or (*b*) such "narrowness, closeness, or bad arrangement . . . of the streets and houses, . . . or the want of light, air, ventilation, or proper conveniences (as are) dangerous or injurious to the health of the inhabitants." On the complaint of at least two Justices of the Peace, or at least twelve rate-payers, such an area must be inspected by the Medical Officer of Health and be reported to the local sanitary authority. If he report that the area is not unhealthy the twelve ratepayers may appeal to the Local Government Board, who will cause an official enquiry.*

When the local authority has decided upon the clearance of such an area it must next prepare an improvement scheme which the Local Government Board confirms by a provisional order. The local authority may then demolish all property that it

---

* It is important to note here that the medical officer has only to show that there are conditions in the area of complaint "*dangerous to health*," and not necessarily that illness is then being directly caused by those conditions. Thus, in the case of overcrowding, he has only to demonstrate that so many persons inhabit such and such houses in the area that the overcrowding becomes "dangerous to health."

thinks desirable in the area after paying compensation to the owners of such property. But the authorities are responsible for re-housing (in London) at least half of the ejected inhabitants, or such proportion as the Local Government Board shall determine.

**Part II.** Part II., which applies to all urban and rural sanitary authorities (the London boroughs and rural districts must seek ratification of the County Council above them), provides a means of dealing with small slum areas. The Medical Officer of Health, whose duty it is to inspect all districts under his charge, or any four ratepayers, may report on such houses as they consider to be "unfit for human habitation" to the local sanitary authority. The authority may then apply for a closing order at the Petty Sessions (the owner has an appeal to the Quarter Sessions), and, in the last resort, obtain an order for demolition. It may also remove obstructive dwellings, such as back to back houses, etc., and reconstruct dwellings on an improvement scheme,* which, however, requires the ratification of the Local Government Board. The somewhat difficult legal procedure causes this part of the Act to be but little used, although it confers some real benefits.

**Part III.** Part III., the most valuable part of the Act for practical housing reform, enables local

---

* In the case of *rural* districts improvement schemes can *only* be carried out under Part II. of the Act ; thus also with London Borough Councils. But County Councils and all Urban District Councils outside London may proceed under Parts I. *or* II.

sanitary authorities to erect workers' dwellings
whenever they consider it necessary to do so, and
without any clearance of other areas. This part
of the Act may be adopted (and this must be done
by an official resolution) by the London County
Council and all *urban* sanitary authorities; *rural*
authorities must seek ratification of any schemes
for building from the County Council of their
district. The land required for such building may
be compulsorily purchased, which generally
implies 10% on the market value as compensation.
In case of dispute over this price, the Local
Government Board is to appoint an arbitrator to
decide the question. The land thus purchased
may be either let to builders, or a company of
builders, or be built upon by the local authority
itself. Gardens attaching to such houses must not
be more than half an acre in extent; and the
houses themselves may be supplied, if the authority
think fit, with all necessary fittings and even fully
furnished (sec. 59). The local authority may,
instead of erecting new houses, purchase or recon-.
struct such houses already existing as might be
suitable for workers' dwellings. And by the
amending Act of 1900, the necessary land required
may be purchased *within or without* the district of
the local sanitary authority.

The money necessary for such schemes, if the
amount does not exceed two years' rateable value
in the district, may be raised in the following
ways :—(*a*) The London County Council may
create consolidated stock repayable within sixty

years; but the leave of the Treasury has first to be obtained; (*b*) Urban District Councils and Town Councils may either borrow of the Public Works Department or create stock with the rates as security. The repayment in either case must be within sixty years. Part IV. of the Act has an important clause directed against corruption in the various local councils. Parts V. and VI. concern Scotland and Ireland especially, whilst the last part (Part VII.) contains only technical details.

4.—The Small Dwellings Acquisition Act. The only other Act of Parliament which we need mention in any detail is the Small Dwellings Acquisition Act of 1899. This Act gives local authorities power to loan money to persons who wish to become the owners of their own (small) houses. This Act may be adopted by any Borough, Urban District, or Rural District Council with jurisdiction over a population of not less than 10,000 persons. When the population is less than 10,000 the local authority must receive the consent of the County Council (or, failing this, the Local Government Board) for the adoption of the Act. Four-fifths of the purchase money, which must not exceed £400, may be thus advanced to residents or intending residents only, and the rate of interest is to be not more than $\frac{1}{4}$% more than the rate at which the council receives its loan from the Public Works Department. Repayments must be made at least every six months and must end within thirty years. Certain conditions as to the use of the house thus being purchased are imposed, *e.g.* it must not be used for the sale of drink. It must be kept in good repair by the resident, who signs a document vesting the ownership in the Council until total payment for the purchase has been made. The resident, however, may transfer his interest in the house under proper conditions of transfer. The Act for various reasons has been little used. Only about a dozen authorities have adopted the Act, and far the largest amount sanctioned has been in the case of the Ilford Urban District Council, which has borrowed over £20,000 under the Act.

5.—The London Building Act. For the law concerning building regulations we have, for the metropolis, the London Building Act of 1894, which consolidates all previous Acts; the bye-laws of the London County Council are also, of course, to be observed in London. In all other districts the local bye-laws impose various building conditions, drawn up in accordance with the model bye-laws of the Local Government Board. Many of our large towns have special local Acts which affect, in many cases very importantly, the districts over which they have jurisdiction. Rural districts' bye-laws, however, must be sanctioned by the County Council; but in many cases there are none in existence.

6.—Powers under Existing Acts. These, then, are the main points of the English law on Housing. By it, as we have seen, any individual may make formal complaint to the local authority as to the insanitary conditions of his own or any other person's house, and amongst these insanitary conditions is expressly included over-crowding. By it also any twelve ratepayers may claim special inspection of any area dangerous to the public health, and its condemnation if it be shown to be unhealthy; they may appeal to the Local Government Board if their claim be dis-regarded by the local sanitary authority. And, again, by it the occupier of any of the workers' dwellings as described in the various Acts, may compel his landlord to put the house into such order and repair as to be "fit for human habitation." If compelled to leave such a house because of its insanitary condition he may also claim for removal expenses. Lastly, the worker tenant may borrow from the local authority, if it have adopted the Small Dwellings Acquisition Act, the greater part of the purchase money wherewith to purchase the house in which he lives.

By these laws the powers of the local authorities in housing matters are considerable. As we have also seen, a Town Council, by means of its various committees, may (1) close and demolish insanitary houses with the widest discretion; (2) inspect all new buildings, compelling them to conform to the local bye-laws on building. Both the Sanitary Inspector and the Medical Officer of Health, with their subordinates, have large powers in this con-nection. And (3) a Town Council may erect houses, within or without the town area, for the better housing of the people.

7.—**Defects of Existing Legislation.** All

this, then, *may* be done. But how much actually
has been done or is being done? The answer to this
question will appear as we attempt to deal with the
various remedies and the success which they have
attained. Undoubtedly much has been done in all
our larger cities and in many of our smaller towns
for the improvement of the public health, and the
lower death-rates are a convincing proof of this
praiseworthy advance.

But it must not be thought that the existing
legislation, even when well administered, is by
any means perfect. The Act of 1890 left much
to be desired even with the amending Acts of 1900
and 1903. In the first place, it is not yet decided
beyond dispute how far the powers of the local
authorities go towards purchasing land *" against
future needs."* It is true that an assurance was
given when the 1890 Act was in Committee by the
then President of the Local Government Board
that "there would be no limitation in the power of
purchase, so long as it was for the purpose and
subject to the provisions of the Bill." Still, this is
not made plain in the Act, and it is a most important point, for on this power of purchasing land
"against future needs" outside our towns largely
depends the future planning out of those towns by
the local authorities. In other words, there is
concerned here the whole question of town development, one of the most important of all questions
to housing reformers.

Then, again, the procedure necessary under the
1890 Act was altogether too intricate, especially in

the case of the rural districts. By that Act a
Parish Council, before it could build workers'
dwellings, had to appeal to the Rural District
Council to take the matter up. The Rural District
Council was obliged to obtain a certificate from
the County Council giving permission to adopt
Part III. of the Act. Then the Rural District
Council must wait for a new election of its
members before adopting any building scheme.
Consent of the Local Government Board and a
special Act of Parliament had also to be obtained
to compulsorily purchase the required land. It is
true that the 1900 Act considerably simplifies this
procedure, for the certificate from the County
Council is no longer necessary and the Parish
Council now has the County Council as a Court of
Appeal in case of the resistance of a lethargic or
hostile Rural District Council, an extremely important provision. There is still, however, a
" prodigality of precaution " * which simply tends
to no action being taken by many local authorities.
There should be the same powers of compulsory
purchase given to the Parish Council for building
as it already possesses for allotments. (Sec. 9 of
the Local Government Act, 1894.) Mr. Walter
Crotch suggests that the preliminary enquiry in
such cases should rest with the Local Government
Board direct and not, as now, with the County

* Cf. W. Walter Crotch, "Cottage Homes," chap. x. He
declares (p. 37) : " Few will be unprepared for the remark
that the Housing of the Working Classes Act, 1890, is, so
far as rural districts are concerned, an almost complete
failure."

Council; then there would be, he maintains, "an immense simplification of procedure."*

There is yet another serious defect in one of the main provisions of the 1890 Act—it is the short time in which repayments of loans must be made. At present eighty years is the outside limit for the London County Council and Urban District Councils within which repayment must be effected, and only fifty years for London Borough Councils. In the rural districts the period of repayment is even shorter—thirty to thirty-five years in the case of leasehold land, forty years in the case of freehold. It is difficult to see the reason for these short periods for repayment which are a serious bar to reform. There is perhaps no change which is more needed in the administration of our housing laws. As we shall see later, it is oftentimes the crux of the whole matter in the case of the municipal building of workers' dwellings. "The advantage to a building authority of being able to extend the repayment of the principal and interest over a period of sixty, eighty, or even a hundred years with land as an asset, would be incalculable. So long as the members of rural authorities are dominated by the fear that the provision of cottage accommodation will send up the rates of the area in which they live, so long will they be found indifferent to the most crying needs."†

8.—**Committee on Repayment of Loans (1902).** This matter was the subject of a Committee, appointed by Parliament, in 1902, on the

* Cf. p. 149.     † Crotch, chap. x.

c

motion of Dr. T. J. Macnamara. The Committee recommended that the period for repayment should be extended, in the case of sites for dwellings, to eighty years, and, in the case of building loans, to sixty years as maximum. But the results of this Committee were practically nil. In the same year an influential deputation, consisting of representatives from nearly all the local authorities in the country, was received by the President of the Local Government Board (May 28th, 1902). It asked (1) that only *one* inquiry should be necessary when a local authority had applied for an improvement scheme; (2) that closing orders might be issued without the order of the magistrates; (3) that the Local Government Board should be sufficient to authorise compulsory purchase of land for workers' dwellings without having recourse to Parliament; and (4) that the customary 10 per cent. over market value for compulsory purchase should no longer be granted. In this case, also, no definite action resulted.

On November 6th of last year another deputation of housing reformers of every shade of opinion, under the auspices of the National Housing Reform Council, waited upon the Prime Minister and President of the Local Government Board. This deputation was sympathetically received, and Sir Henry Campbell-Bannerman declared his intention of giving effect, so far as possible, to the recommendations and suggestions made to him on that occasion.

# CHAPTER III.

----

" The evils arising out of overcrowding will never be successfully grappled with until it is fully realised that the root of the problem lies in the diminution or stagnation of population that has for years past characterised rural districts." (*Select Committee on Housing of the Working Classes Acts Amendment Bill*, 1906.)

----

DURING the second half of the Nineteenth Century there was consummated the great change, in the economic life of England, which is known as the Industrial Revolution. Until that time England had been an agricultural and stock-breeding country, her rural districts occupied, for the most part, by a stout yeoman class and a hard-working peasant community. The landed aristocracy had large estates in the country districts, but many of these were sub-let to the yeoman and small farmers in various sized holdings. Gradually these holdings were surrendered or sold, and the land passed into the hands of a comparatively few owners. This change is

27

still going on to the detriment of both town and country. Our rural districts are becoming more and more depopulated, the rate of exodus from country to town being at least 150,000 per annum. It has been computed that during the years 1871-91 as many as 500,000 wage-earners left the rural districts to reside in industrial centres; whilst in the twenty years (1881-1901) the number of agricultural labourers declined from 984,000 to 689,000, and no less than 244 new urban districts were created.

1.—**Causes of the Rural Exodus.** Many causes have been suggested to account for this remarkable exodus from the country to the towns. It is, of course, no new tendency, for even in Tudor times we find in the attack then made on the " common lands " system the first beginning of this migration, but it is only in recent years that the movement to the town has become such a menace to our national life.

We are now confronted with the fact that England is rapidly becoming an industrial country. As wool producing was found to be a more prosperous undertaking than corn growing in the Tudor times, so now our coal and manufactures pay better than our farming. Meanwhile agriculture, still our largest industry, has been sadly hindered by unjust legislation and the conservatism of the farmers.

A very important cause of the present rural depopulation is what is generally known as the " Land Question." That four-fifths of the land

of the United Kingdom should be in the possession of some 7,000 landowners is a very serious
hindrance to rural prosperity.* This fact means
that the agricultural labourer has no "stake in the
soil," no profitable interest in the land, and is
consequently at the mercy of the squire and large
landowner. While it is true that industrial
causes have attracted labourers to the towns, it is
equally true that for the agricultural labourers in
the rural districts there is no hope either of
independence during their working years or of a
sufficiency in their old age. It may be impossible
altogether to stem the great stream of workers
from country to town in modern industrial
England, but, at least, it should be possible to
offer counter-attractions in the country. In
Denmark, during the last half century, the exodus
has not only been checked, but the tide has to
some extent actually turned in the opposite
direction. This has been accomplished by a great
national effort, which has shown itself in a remarkable system of agricultural education and co-
operation, aided by the establishment of small
holdings in all parts of the country. No less than
five-sixths of Danish land is now held by free-
holders and peasants in this way. Legislation
in England, directed to the promotion of small
holdings and of better housing, by placing compulsory powers in the hands of local bodies, has
not been altogether successful for a variety of
reasons, and the time has come for a fresh attempt.

* "Land Reform" (Rt. Hon. Jesse Collings), p. 86.

This is not the place to advocate land reform in detail, but until something is done in this direction rural depopulation is not likely to be seriously stayed. The Report of the Select Committee on the Rural Housing Bill,* that of the Small Holdings Committee, and Mr. R. H. Rew's Report to the Board of Agriculture, all point in the same direction.

2.—**The House Famine.** But there is another cause for this depopulation, perhaps only subsidiary, but of the utmost importance, especially at this time, and that is the present condition of rural housing. Akin to the lack of small holdings is this lack of cheap house accommodation. Cottages at cheaper rents and in greater numbers must be forthcoming or the process of depopulation will continue. No decent cottages, with land attached, are to be had in many of our rural districts to-day. The evidence of Miss Constance Cochrane, who has devoted much time to this particular part of the problem is, " We are still compelled to recognise the unhappy fact that the question of how to house in a suitable and sanitary manner (at their present wages) all those who would like to remain in the villages scattered by hundreds up and down the country has not been solved."† There is undoubtedly a house famine in the rural districts, and this, partly at least, accounts for the continued drift of population from the country to town.

* To be obtained of Wyman & Sons, Fetter Lane, E.C. (1/-).
† See a paper in the *Sanitary Record*, October 5th, 1905.

We may also quote official witnesses. " The Committee (on Housing of the Working Classes Acts Amendment Bill, 1906) have had abundant evidence before them as to the insufficiency of cottages in rural districts. Cases have been brought to their notice in which people have had to leave a village because of the lack of house accommodation, while others have been prevented from coming to live in a district because no house or cottage was to be found fit to live in. . . . The house famine in town and country, which often exists in regard to the working classes, is incontestable." And a recent writer calls attention to " the increasing difficulty of young men and women finding comfortable homes in the village of their birth, and the accentuation which this difficulty gives to the already too great tendency to migrate to the town."

3.—**Defective and Insanitary Housing in Rural Districts.** This evil is intensified by the terribly insanitary state of the existing accommodation. Whilst the standard of general living has been steadily rising in the country during the last half-century, that of rural housing seems to have as steadily fallen. The Select Committee just referred to confirm this. " A higher standard of living throughout the country has correspondingly increased the demand among the younger generation for a better-class cottage, with more accommodation and space than the older generation was content with. This demand has not been met in most districts."*

* Select Committee's Report, § 25.

To quote Miss Cochrane again :—

" As a member of the Rural Housing and Sanitation Association, and as one who has for many years been intimately conversant with the homes of the agricultural poor, I have seen— together with their usual accompaniments of ill-health, low morals, and general discomfort— conditions which are a disgrace to a nation which calls itself Christian, and professes to be guided by the principles of Christianity." . . .

" I have seen men, women, and children living in houses without a water supply anywhere near, or with only polluted supplies quite unfit to drink. I have seen leaking roofs, floors and walls saturated with damp, papers and carpets peeling and mildewed, unceiled ceilings with dirty thatch dropping on to furniture and beds; storm water flowing through living rooms ; bedrooms small, close, crowded, and with tiny windows nearly on the floor level ; larders merely dark cupboards opening into living rooms; foul and worn-out sanitary conveniences shared by several families ; rotten floors incapable of supporting beds ; windows that do not open ; wide crevices round badly-fitting outer doors; broken and uneven brick floors ; and many other discomforts, such as no coppers or cupboards, and thick mud up to and around houses " (the *Sanitary Record*, December 28th, 1905).

A Sussex Sanitary Inspector, Mr. Brice Phillips, reports as follows :—" If the construction and general sanitary state of the houses are deplorable, much more so are the conditions existing among the inmates. A typical case was a house containing two bedrooms. In a small room of barely 300 cubic feet capacity slept the occupier, his housekeeper and one of her children. The remaining room, of 750 cubic feet, was devoid of furniture except one dilapidated bedstead, covered indifferently with dirty bed-linen. At an inspection—a surprise visit—there was clear evidence that this room, with its one bed, had been occupied at the same time by two sons, aged 23 and 12 years, and two daughters aged 20 and 6 years respectively."

It may be objected that these are isolated instances of neglected house property, only typical of the district for which the witness speaks ; but the evidence of Mr. W. Walter Crotch confirms these statements :—

" During 1897 a London association conducted a systematic inquiry in 78 villages, having 4,179 cottages. Of these nearly one quarter were in such a state as to be described as ' bad ' or ' extremely bad.' Sixty per cent. had no fire-places in any bedroom, and, therefore, could have no proper and necessary ventilation. Proper nursing in cases of sickness, under these conditions, it is obvious, becomes an absolute impossibility. In 15 per cent. of the cottages referred to, the water supply was either very bad, or there was none. Another inquiry extended over 240 villages and about 10,000 dwellings. In half of these villages the cottages were ' bad,' and in some 30 villages there were cases of gross overcrowding."*

* " Cottage Homes of England," pp. 7 and 8.

**4.—Causes of House Famine.** The reasons for this lack of house room are not difficult to discover. In the first place there has been a steady diminution, so far as the original supply of workmen's cottages is concerned. Owing to the drift of population into the towns, not only did the landowner cease to construct more cottages, but many of the existing buildings were demolished and the supply thus considerably lessened.

" Farms in many parts of the country have gradually given place to park land, grazing grounds, and shooting estates, and the only class of people who have increased in numbers in the country are gamekeepers, for whom not many cottages need to be provided. At an early period the Poor Law rates, being chargeable to the parish instead of to the district, as is now the case, appear to have been the cause of many cottages being pulled down in order to avoid the heavy expenses connected with this rate."*

Another writer says :—

" While the depopulation of country villages has been rapid, the falling into decay of the cottages has been more rapid still. In a purely agricultural district it is a rare sight to see new cottages being built, for of late years there has been a general cessation in the building of cottages for agricultural labourers."†

In the second place, the supply which has thus

---

* Dr. Simpson, " Rural Housing and the Bye-laws connected therewith."

† Miss Churton, the *Sanitary Record*, May 26th, 1904.

been diminished by want of repair and by demolition is not likely to be increased by private enterprise. Wages are so low in our agricultural
districts (13s. per week in *cash* wages is the average
in England!) that a rent cannot be paid by
labourers sufficient to remunerate the investor of
money in cottage building. £130 will be found to
be the very least capital outlay on a suitable
cottage for a labourer and family, and the interest
at 4% on this demands a rent of 2s. a week, or
roughly £5 a year. Most rural landlords are glad
to get as much as £4 a year, and even then they
undertake to meet all expenses for repairs and
perhaps pay the rates as well. The speculating
builder is not likely to build under these conditions,
as the Royal Commission on Labour admitted.
"The rent which is received for cottage property
in rural districts is not sufficient to make the building of good cottages directly profitable."*

5.—"Tied Cottage" System.† Nor can the
landowner be trusted to increase or to improve the

---

* Mr. W. C. Little in the "Royal Commission on Labour,"
Vol. v., Part i., p. 123.

† Cf. Report of Mr. R. Farrar, L.G.B. Inspector, for
Durham Rural District (1905). "In the colliery villages
the great majority of dwellings are owned by the colliery
companies and assigned by them to their employees, who are
not required to pay rent, a deduction under this head, however, being made from their wages. This method of letting
operates in some respects to the disadvantage of the
employees, who are debarred of free choice in respect of
their residences and who, naturally, do not take the same
interest in the upkeep of houses thus assigned to them, as
they would in respect of dwellings taken by themselves."

present supply. It is certain that when he is the small farmer who sub-lets "tied cottages" to his labourers, the system is far from satisfactory. "Out of job, out of house," is the hopeless watchword of such a tenantry. These landowners complain that it does not pay to properly house their labourers. The reason is obvious. "Cottage building does *not* pay, for the simple and sufficient reason that it never was intended to pay, any more than the farmhouse or the cowshed was intended to provide a remunerative investment in itself. The labourer's wages have never included a sum for economic rent, and if the building of cottages does not pay, it is because the labourer who inhabits them gets his lodgings, wholly or in part, in lieu of wages."\* So that the whole problem of rural housing really resolves itself into the old question of "a living wage." With wages as low as they are at present, part of which are really paid in free or nominal rents, no outlay in cottage building will yield a fair return. Thus not only is the form of tenantry oftentimes unsatisfactory, eviction following on loss of employment, but there is no inducement to the landlords to supply sufficient cottages or to keep the existing supply in decent repair.

6.—Results of House Famine. The effects of this rural house famine press very hardly on those who still inhabit our villages. It means first, of course, that there is much overcrowding in the

---

\* " Towards a Social Policy," chap. iii.

existing cottages. This is as real an evil as is the
overcrowding in many of our largest cities to-day.
During the inquiry for the purpose of erecting
cottages at Ixworth (Suffolk) it was officially
declared : "the ground itself seems overcrowded
with hovels (they can scarcely be called houses,
how much less homes?), and these hovels are
themselves sometimes overcrowded with inhabitants." In the Autumn of 1899 the *Daily News*
instituted a careful inquiry into rural housing
conditions in the South and West of England, and
Mr. Clement Edwards, M.P., was sent as a Special
Commissioner to gather first-hand evidence. Here
is an extract from his report, after he had visited
the rural districts in this part of our country :—

"It is not only that the cottages are in a horrible
state of decay and disrepair. That is bad enough
in all conscience. But even worse is the appalling
manner in which they are so often overcrowded.
Some of the facts that I gleaned were positively
revolting in themselves, and much worse in their
obvious suggestion of inevitable social and moral
results. In one part of Wiltshire alone, during my
necessarily brief inquiry, I came across fifteen
instances where more than five people are occupying one small bedroom; ten cases where more than
six ; eight, more than seven ; six, more than
eight ; three, more than nine ; two, more than ten ;
and one where eleven people are sleeping in a
single bedroom. In a single district of Somerset-
shire, in one day, I was shown half-a-dozen
cottages with two little bedrooms, accommodating

a couple of lodgers—single labourers as a rule—in addition to the members of the family." *

Another effect of this scarcity of supply is that rents are forced up beyond the means of the ordinary agricultural labourer. The wages, as we have seen, are much too small to allow of a proper economic rent, and yet he is faced with, at least, two or three shillings a week for his cottage. Either he has to be content with very inferior accommodation at the small rent he can afford to pay, or he receives, as we have also seen, the whole or part of his rent free at the hands of his employer. This generally means either servility on the part of the labourer or summary eviction, sometimes at a week's notice. In this latter case he is despoiled of all the value of the work put into the land attaching to the cottage, a very common grievance in our rural districts. Another obvious effect of this scarcity of accommodation is that when once a cottage at a moderate rent has been obtained, all sorts of insanitary conditions will be quietly submitted to before the inhabitants will surrender their home.

7.—A Minimum Standard. What, then, is the standard of cottage accommodation which we ought to set up in our rural districts? In a paper, read at the Rural Housing Reform Conference at the Garden City, Letchworth, in September, 1906, Miss Cochrane asserted: "I have during the past few weeks visited the homes

* Cf. "The House Famine and How to relieve it." Fabian Tract, No. 101. Paper I.

of fifty labourers' wives—taken as they came—at fairly regular intervals, throughout six villages and a hamlet in the counties of Cambridgeshire, Huntingdonshire, and a corner of Bedfordshire. From each of these, separately, I have ascertained exactly how they would build their cottages if a kind fairy presented them with £150 or £200 for the purpose." This investigation elicited the following facts. There was an almost universal desire for *three* bedrooms, and many statements were made to the effect that this was the least possible number. "Nearly all would be satisfied with a fireplace in one bedroom, but a few would like one in two rooms. In every instance the women asked for a sitting-room and a kitchen living-room on the ground floor, and all, except six, wished the kitchen to be about 15 ft. long by 12 ft. to 15 ft. wide." In reference to this much debated sitting-room or parlour, another recent writer has pertinently remarked, "The woman who takes in sewing or washing will use such a room for storing her clean, finished work, as well as her sewing machine, if she has one, her little treasures also, or anything she wants to keep out of the way of the children or the soil of household work. If it is useful for no other purpose, it is, at all events, a place in which a coffin may be placed; perhaps the mention of such an eventuality may bring home to those who have never thought of it, the difficulties of those who have to live in a cottage with only one living room where there is any aspiration to preserve the decencies of life."

The verdict of the women on other matters was as follows:—"The large majority would like the copper and sink in a shed outside, which should also contain a small fireplace, just to hold a kettle or saucepan for cooking in summer. The desire for brick floors in the kitchen and wooden floors in the sitting-room was almost unanimous, and all, excepting two, would like one large sash window in every room. . . . All wished for a larder or pantry. Rather less than half would care for a bath, and others would be satisfied to continue the use of the wash-tub."

8.—**The Model Cottage.** The model cottage, then, must have (1) a sufficient number of convenient, well-built rooms; (2) it also must have a good space of land behind and in front, not only to include the minimum $\frac{1}{4}$-acre of garden which helps to pay the rent, but also furnishes the necessary space for drainage and ventilation. It has been urged that the minimum space of 24 ft. in front and 15 ft. behind, prescribed by the Model Bye-laws of 1903 for houses not exceeding 35 ft. in height, is hardly sufficient. Even if it were sufficient for urban building it is not sufficient for rural housing, since space has to be left for drainage and disposal of refuse; also for the well which must be entirely free from pollution from any source. It is the opinion of many that one quarter of an acre is the minimum quantity of land required.

(3) This model cottage must be built of cheap but good materials. A recent writer on this matter asserts, " I think it is very desirable to demonstrate

that it is possible to build for a cost of about £150 a country labourer's cottage with all reasonable requirements, which shall at the same time be well-built and shall not be an eyesore on the landscape."* This writer, recognising the importance of illustration in discussions of this kind, gives a concrete example of his own to prove the point. " I have myself a plan which I have used as a model for labourers' cottages at Brandsby, in the N. Riding of Yorkshire. This cottage has been built for £150, and special care has been taken with the quality of the work and construction. I am quite satisfied from my own experience that a country builder, who works on the job with his men, can build these cottages in pairs for a price varying from £140 to £160 each, according to circumstances." This model cottage, as the plan shows, contains a kitchen-living-room, 15 ft. by 12 ft., a parlour, 12 ft. by 9 ft., a scullery, larder, porch, three bedrooms (with fireplace in each) and all conveniences.

" What I have tried to show," he adds, " is that it is possible to build such a cottage as a labourer can live in decently and comfortably *for a sum that will bring in a reasonable return either directly or indirectly.*"

9.—**Rural Councils and Labourers' Cottages.** Can the local authorities supply such cottages ? Judging from the attempts that have already been made, it seems as though it were

* See article by Mr. Fairfax Cholmeley in the *Builder* for December 30th, 1905.

D

impossible without further extending their powers and amending the existing legislation. In the agricultural districts just where the rent-paying capacity of the worker is lowest, we find the administrative difficulties in connection with municipal housing to be greatest. A local authority attempts to adopt Part III. of the Housing of the Working Classes Act, and finds it not only extremely expensive, but also a very cumbrous piece of machinery, while the rate of interest on loans instead of being low, is unnecessarily high.

Only two rural District Councils have built cottages, and in neither case with marked success, for the reasons we have already stated. The Ixworth (Suffolk) cottages were built as a result of the action taken by the Labourers' Association, which applied to the Suffolk County Council for assistance. The Rural Sanitary Authority was compelled to take action under the Public Health Act, and Part II. of the Housing Act of 1890. The supply of cottages was not only insanitary but inadequate, and consequently it was necessary to build. A County Council inquiry was held, and the adoption of Part III. of the Act of 1890 was sanctioned, the expenses to fall upon the whole rural district rather than on the parish of Ixworth. The Rural District Council objected to this, and appealed to the County Council for another inquiry. The appeal was granted and the former decision reversed. The Labourers' Association then appealed to the Local Government Board, and the Local Government Board referred the matter back to the County Council, and finally the County Council, at the instigation of Lord F. Hervey who held the original inquiry, gave their consent. In 1892 a new Sanitary Authority was elected, which adopted Part III. of the Housing Act, bought four acres of land, and built eight cottages at a total cost of £1,700. The money was borrowed at 3¼ per cent. for thirty years, so that the loan charges amounted to about £10 10s. a year for each cottage. The cottages are let for £5 5s. a year (4s. 5d. extra being paid for an allotment of garden ground) so that each cottage loses £5 5s. per annum. Cheaper money and a longer term of years might have obviated this loss.

In the case of the Penshurst (Kent) Cottages, the obstacles to success were apathy, vested interests, and the usual cumbrous procedure. The struggle lasted from 1895 to 1899, and the cottages were built in 1900. Six cottages were constructed at a cost of £1,800, and the money borrowed at 3¼ per cent. from the Public Works Loan Commissioners for a period of forty years. The rents are 5s. a week, which is far more than an agricultural labourer can afford to pay. It is now proposed to build an additional six cottages, which it is hoped will cost less than the first experiment.

These two illustrations alone are sufficient to indicate some of the difficulties that housing reformers have to meet with in the country.

Only nine applications in all have been made

under Part III., and this neglect is attributed by the Select Committee on the " Housing of the Working Classes Acts Amendment Bill, 1906," largely to financial difficulties, since many District Councils are deterred from building by the fear of a loss and the consequent burden upon the rates.

10.—Recommendations of Select Committee (1906). However true this may be of the construction of houses, it is no excuse for the neglect by the Rural District Councils of their duties in the sanitary inspection of existing houses, and the Select Committee recommends that the whole administration of the Public Health Acts in rural districts be transferred to the County Councils. With regard to the administration of the Housing Acts, the Committee recommends that it also be transferred to the County Council * with the proviso that the Rural District Councils should have concurrent power to provide additional houses under Part III., subject to confirmation by the Local Government Board. It is not improbable that with facilities in the way of loans at low rates of interest, the Rural District Councils might manifest more activity in this

* The Committee give five reasons for concluding that " the Rural District Councils are less favourably circumstanced than the County Councils for carrying out this work." (1) The small area of the former makes heavier charges upon the rates. (2) A central body like the County Council could build better and more cheaply. (3) It could raise larger, and, therefore, cheaper loans. (4) There would thus result "a closer uniformity of administration in the County generally." (5) The County Council is a more desirable authority to deal with the compulsory purchase of land, § 58.

direction. The Committee further proposes that the County Councils should appoint Statutory Public Health and Housing Committees, and that the Local Government Board should have a separate department dealing with this subject, together with an adequate staff of travelling sanitary and housing inspectors. The keeping of a register of survey of all buildings, and the requirement of an annual return from owners of house property would also follow these two proposals.

As regards the provision of additional house accommodation, the Committee emphasize two points in particular: (1) the desirability of providing cottages, *with land attached;* and (2) the necessity of loans for housing being granted by the Treasury at lower rates than has hitherto been the case. As regards (1), the Committee point out that though allotments are fairly universal, they are often at some distance from the labourer's cottage; and that, where land adjoining a cottage has been provided, it has been found possible to let the cottage and land to a superior class of labourer at a fair rent. The Committee recommend the abolition, as soon as practicable, of the " tied cottage " system, to which we have already referred.

In respect of (2), the granting of loans by the Treasury at lower rates, the Committee consider that cottages cannot be erected in purely agricultural districts, however cheaply, at such a price as to cover interest, sinking fund and repairs, and admit of the rent being within the means of a labourer under existing circumstances. Grants or subventions of some kind are therefore necessary, and the Committee recommend that these grants take the form of Treasury loans at the lowest rate for which they themselves could borrow, and that the period of redemption should be extended to sixty or eighty years, without any increase in the rate of interest. Under the present system the rate of interest rises with the length of period over which the loan extends. What is the object of all this if the Treasury has the security of rates to fall back on? The Post Office pays 2½ per cent. interest on £150,000,000 of working-class savings, the Treasury asks 4½ per cent. on loans with which to build cottages for the same people. Why not use the working-class savings for this purpose, charging say an extra half per cent. to cover expenses of administration?

One other difficulty, which local authorities will meet in any endeavour to supply the demand for decent cottages, will be the inflated value of the land purchased compulsorily for building purposes. The Committee declares that, "No solution will be satisfactory that does not enable a local authority to purchase land compulsorily for any public purpose (including housing, drainage, small holdings, &c.), upon the basis of its rateable value. The present system under which land is rated by a local authority upon one valuation, but can only be purchased by the same authority upon another valuation, having no necessary or recognised proportion to the first, seems both complicated and unjust."

If these recommendations could be embodied in an amendment to the existing law, it seems probable, if not certain, that a marked improvement in the housing conditions of .the agricultural labourers would speedily follow.

# CHAPTER IV.

"The Huns and Vandals who will destroy the
Christian states of Europe are being bred not in the
wilds of Asia but in the slums of our great cities."

(MACAULAY.)

## 1.—Growth of the City.

WE have forgotten how to live in the country,
and we have not yet learnt how to live in
the town, and meanwhile our towns and cities are
growing with immense rapidity. According to the
1901 census (England and Wales) 77 per cent. of
our population (25,054,628) live in urban sanitary
districts, as compared with 75 per cent. in 1891.
A hundred years ago the conditions were reversed,
and two-thirds of the population lived in the
country. In 1801, 16 per cent. of the people lived
in towns of over 20,000 ; in 1901, 59 per cent. !
The tendency still continues, and since we cannot
do away with city life we must attempt to lessen
its evils or at all events its "unnecessary
miseries." It is here that we really come to the
crux of the whole question. The city to-day is

48

the point at which all the worst features of
defective and inadequate housing accommodation
focus themselves. Mr. Charles Booth, to whose
work we shall have to make constant reference,
actually goes so far as to declare that it is " the
supreme question of the day in London." This
verdict is in perfect agreement with that of a
recent writer who declares that "the housing
problem of the cities is at once the most insistent
and the most complex of all the problems immedi-
ately facing the social reformer." *

First let us notice that this problem of housing
in our cities affects not only the " poorest poor,"
but all sections of the people who earn a small
weekly or monthly wage. It has been pointed out
how true this is, particularly of the central part of
our great Metropolis. "Thus it comes about
that the people who live within inner London are
housed as a class worse than their means would
indicate. The artisan who is not really poor is
yet poorly housed; the labourer who is poor, but
not very poor, is yet very poorly housed." †

"No room to live *healthily* !" if not "No room
to live!" may indeed be written large across most
of our cities and towns to-day. All sections of the
working-class, people who need the freedom and
health of a good, roomy house quite as much, if
not more, than the leisured classes of society,
suffer severe physical disability as regards housing
accommodation.

* " Towards a Social Policy," chap. x.
† " Heart of the Empire: The Housing Problem."

2.—**Overcrowding per Acre.** There are two kinds of overcrowding, corresponding to the first two points of the problem as stated in our introductory chapter. (1) Too many houses must not be built on any given area of land; (2) Too many people must not live in any one room or house. These are two distinct evils. In London the great evil is overcrowding of people per room and per house; in Manchester it is overcrowding and bad arrangement of houses on a given area. Both these evils are frequently found in the same town and both must be attacked if the problem is to be solved. (1) Taking, first, then, the overcrowding of houses on areas, we must give some definition which will enable us to estimate this sort of overcrowding. We find the true test is to ascertain the number of persons per acre. The late Sir Benjamin Richardson held that no city could be in a properly healthy condition which had more than twenty-five people to the acre. Adopting this as our standard, what is the condition of affairs in some of our cities? Let us take York as our first example. We find that this city has an average population of 20.5 persons to the acre which we see is a slight improvement on the health standard we have given. It compares very favourably with Manchester and Birmingham where the population per acre is 42.1 and 41.1 respectively, or with South Shields which seems to hold the unenviable distinction, with its fifty-four persons to the acre, of being the worst town in England in this respect. But these figures are very deceptive if we forget the fact that they represent an *average* population distributed over the whole number of acres which form the extent of the city. In York, as in all cities, this population is very unevenly distributed as a glance at the table of the various districts of the city, given in Mr. Rowntree's book on York, will show.* One of these districts, a busy working-class centre, has as many as 349 persons to the acre, another 246, and yet another 237 ! The same story is told of Manchester where in one poor district (Hulme) 141 persons live on each acre, whilst the average for Rusholme, a wealthy suburb, stands at only 15 per acre;† the report of the Medical Officers for Edinburgh (1905) shows that while the ward of St. Leonard's has 254·3 persons per acre with a corresponding death rate, St. Bernard's has only 10·6 and Portobello 5·1. Coming to the Metropolis we find such districts as Shoreditch and Paddington‡ with 180·2 and 106·1 persons to the acre respectively, whilst Lewisham and Hampstead have only 18·1 and 36·1 per acre. Even if we regard the matter from the point of view of the number of *houses* to the acre it seems to make little difference. " There are more than three

* Cf. " Poverty, a Study of Town Life," chap. vi.

† "Housing Conditions in Manchester and Salford," p. 17.

‡ A special inquiry in Paddington (1901) revealed the fact that the total population of a selected area was " *equivalent to a density of 480 persons per statute acre.*" Cf. " Results of House-to-House Inquiry in Clarendon Street Area," p. 3 Paddington Housing Committee).

times as many houses per acre in Soho as in the
wealthy district of Mayfair,"* and this is no
exceptional case.

This congestion of people per acre which we
find in central districts is unfortunately not illegal,
and hence the delay and difficulty in combatting
the evil. All that we can do is to exert a steady
pressure in the right direction, not closing and
demolishing insanitary houses without at the
same time finding outlets to newer and less
crowded districts. The causes of this form of
overcrowding are fairly obvious; there is first the
increasingly high price of all urban land, and in
many cases its extreme scarcity for building
purposes. Side by side with this cause is the
supplanting of residential by commercial houses.
"The cause of overcrowding in London is the
conflict for room, which is always going on between the inhabited house and the business
premises." † Commercial forces tend to focus
themselves at the business centre of every large
city, a fact more noticeable in New York and
Chicago, than in London. Hence the monstrosity
of the "skyscraper" in American cities. Those
who are unfortunate enough to have to live in the
inner ring of any of our large towns have to pay
dearly for the questionable privilege. The burden
of rent often falls most heavily on those who can

* "Life in West London : A Contrast." A. Sherwell.
(Cf. also note on p. 233 of Finsbury M. O. Report, 1905.)

† Vide Fabian Tract No. 101, Part IV.

least afford to bear it. Many of the working classes
have necessarily to live near their occupation in
the heart of the city, and as a result they have to
suffer the many disadvantages which such a life
entails.

3.—**Overcrowding in Houses.** Overcrowding in houses* is an evil attended with even worse
results than overcrowding on areas. Here, however, we are helped by some sort of legal definition.
Overcrowding is considered to exist when the
number of persons to the room is "*more than two.*"
That this definition is by no means complete will
be understood when we realise that it contains
nothing as to the *size* of the room, a very important
consideration. The late Professor Huxley gave
it as his opinion that each adult requires at least
800 cubic ft. of space to himself, that is, the space
represented by a small room of 10 ft. square in
area and 8 ft. in height! In the Model Bye-laws
of the Local Government Board, 400 cubic ft. of
air space is required for every person over ten
years of age in any room, not exclusively used as
a sleeping apartment, and 200 cubic ft. for children
under ten years. In rooms used exclusively for
sleeping the amounts are 300 and 150 respectively.
But Army Regulations require 600 cubic ft. per
head for men in barracks, the Metropolitan Police
require 450 and the Poor Law 500 cubic ft. per

---

* "All the space within the external and party walls of a
building is to be considered a separate house by however
many families, living in distinct tenements or apartments,
it may be occupied." (Census Returns, 1901.)

adult.  It has to be remembered that to keep the
air pure and uncontaminated a system of ventilation much more perfect than is found even in
better-class houses is required; and, indeed, this
last point is an important one, for it is a well-
known fact that ventilation is more and more
neglected the lower we go down in the social
scale.  Mr. Rowntree made an interesting investigation in York as to the number of bedroom
windows open at night time; out of nearly 2,500
houses examined, 10 per cent. of the windows
of the highest class were observed to be open,
of the middle class 5 per cent., whilst of the
poorest class only 3 per cent. were left open.
Considering, then, this lack of ventilation we
ought to allow more, rather than less, than the
minimun of 800 cubic ft. for each adult in our
poorest houses.   Now what is the state of
affairs that we actually find?  And here let us
take, as examples, the same three cities from
which we have previously drawn our illustrations
—York, Manchester and London.  Not only are
there recent and reliable figures for these cities,
but they are representative of our various towns,
York a typical cathedral city, Manchester a huge
industrial centre, London a congeries of towns.
In York, even according to the somewhat defective standard we have just given, "it was found
that 663 families, comprising 4,705 persons, were
living under overcrowded conditions. . . .  This
is equal to 10·1 per cent. of the working-class
population or 6·4 per cent. of the total population

of the city." Mr. Rowntree also further qualifies
this testimony by the words : "It must also be
remembered that in the majority of houses only
half the rooms are bedrooms (64 per cent. of
York houses have only two bedrooms), and therefore during the night the *actual* number of persons
per room in these overcrowded houses exceeds *four* ;
in other words the air space is less than 300 cubic ft.
for each person."

In Manchester and Salford out of a total population of 764,829 (1901), 50,790 were living in
overcrowded houses even according to the census
definition. "Here again attention must be drawn
to the fact that in a two-roomed house the whole
family sleeps in one bedroom, and that in a three-
roomed house with six inhabitants, which by
Census standard is not overcrowded, overcrowding
will almost certainly take place every night."*

Turning now to the Metropolis we find that out
of the total population in 1891, 31.5 per cent. was
found to be living under crowded conditions.
There were then 172,502 one-room tenements,† of
which over 27,000 were occupied by four or more
than four persons ; in a total of more than a
hundred cases by nine, ten, eleven and even

---

*Cf. "Housing Conditions in Manchester and Salford,"
p. 56. T. R. Marr.

† No less than 18 per cent. of the London tenements con-
sisted (1891) of one room only, but even this proportion is
low in comparison with the 49.5 per cent. of one-roomed
tenements in Stockholm, the 44 per cent. in Berlin and the
37.1 per cent. in Christiania. (Rowntree, "Poverty,"
chap. vi.)

twelve persons in the one room. Fortunately
the census of 1901 shews a slight improvement,
for the figures for that year were only 149,524 one-
room tenements, 17,000 of which were occupied
by four, or more than four persons. As Mr.
Charles Booth says : " These figures indicate
considerable progress in the ten years. . . . In
every way there is considerably less crowding
than ten years ago." Nevertheless, he concludes
a chapter on this subject by declaring : " Of the
insufficiency, badness and dearness of the housing
accommodation available in many parts of London,
I need not say anything more. It would be
difficult to exaggerate the facts."* To give only
one concrete example, of these facts : " In one
street in Southwark, where there are many single
room tenements, it is said that there are eight
hundred people living in thirty-six houses."†

Coming to Finsbury we find that 77 per cent.
of the whole population of the Borough live in
tenements of less than five rooms, 14.3 per cent.
live in homes of one room, whilst 31.2 per cent.
live in homes of two rooms. That is to say, that
45 per cent. of the people of Finsbury live in
homes of two rooms or less, and this Borough is
characterised, more than any other District in
London, by tenement dwellings of less than five
rooms each.‡

* Booth Final Vol. " Life and Labour," p. 180.

† Ibid, p. 174.

‡ Report on Public Health of Finsbury, p. 234, 1905.

And, as if to add to the evils of overcrowding, the unfortunate inhabitants of one or two-room tenements are often engaged in home-trades. Such trades as match-box making, fur-pulling, and even haddock curing are frequently carried on in the one room which the family possesses, thus adding to the pestilential state of the air breathed night and day in this room.

4.—**Causes of Overcrowding.** The causes of this terrible overcrowding in rooms are as easy to discover as they are difficult to remove. Of course, the first is the excessively high rent' which must be paid even for the poorest accommodation in any of our large towns. Here again we may instance from our three selected cities. Mr. Rowntree tells us " that while rent only absorbs 9 per cent. of the total income of the few exceptionally well-to-do working class families earning as much as, or more than, 60s. a week, it absorbs no less than 29 *per cent. of the total income of the very poor,* whose family earnings are under 18s. weekly."* So that if we reckon only those who earn this latter wage, we find that they have to pay a weekly rental averaging over 5s. 2d. per week. Nor are things better in Manchester where even a two-roomed tenement averages 3s. 5d. a week, three-roomed and four-roomed 4s. 3d. and 4s. 1od. respectively.† But it is when we come to London that rent assumes the most serious proportions.

* "Poverty," chap. vi.

† T. R. Marr, " Housing Conditions in Manchester and Salford," chap. iv.

E

" The rents paid by the great mass of London workmen . . . vary between 5s. 6d. and 11s. per week, the most common figures being between 6s. and 8s. per week. The main difference between a workman living outside London and one living nearer the centre consists in the quantity of accommodation rather than in the rent. In very few urban districts can the poor escape with the payment of less than one-fourth of their earnings for rent."* We shall have to return to this question of rent in seeking for remedies to the evils that we are discussing.

Overcrowding as a result of the house famine has already been mentioned and is too obvious to need further illustration, but we must also bear in mind as a secondary cause the habits of the poorest class of tenants, habits which seem to intensify all the evils of slum-dwelling. " Undoubtedly in a certain number of cases overcrowding is due to wasteful expenditure of the household income upon drink and gambling, and there are other cases in which the tenants, although temperate and respectable, appear to be quite content with their overcrowded conditions. . . . With some of these, overcrowding appears to have become a habit. Still, after full allowance has been made for these two causes, there can be no doubt that the cause first named (smallness of income) is by far the most general one." †

* Cf. Thompson, " Housing Handbook," p. 173.
† Rowntree, " Poverty," chap. vi.

**5.—Effect of Slum Environment.** And can we not understand how slum surroundings react upon the habits of the people ? With a single water supply shared, as in Manchester, between twenty, thirty and even forty houses,* what inducement is there to the poor to be clean ? With sanitary conveniences distributed in some cases between four, five and even eight houses,† how great are the difficulties in the way of common decency ! Moreover the general insanitary condition of much of the property occupied by the working-classes tends to expel that " house pride " which is so important a factor in domestic economy. Much of this unhealthy state of the houses is due to bad building. Of one whole district it is said, by one of Mr. Charles Booth's investigators, that " it has been ruined by bad building, having everything else in its favour ; . . . shabby houses are pointed to as the probable slums of the future," . . . houses only up a year, already cracking from roof to front door." ‡ Perhaps the worst feature in the unwholesome environment of the overcrowded parts of our cities is the general dinginess and sordidness which are everywhere apparent ; there is nothing to relieve the hopeless monotony of the long rows of dull, ugly, ill-built houses, " brick boxes with slate lids." Mr. T. C.

---

* T. R. Marr, " Housing in Manchester and Salford," p. 44.

† Ibid p. 46.   Cf. " Poverty," chap. vii.

‡ Booth, Final Vol., pp. 161, 162 : Germany seems to have a special problem in this respect ; *vide* " Example of Germany " (Horsfall), p. 2.

Horsfall has gone so far as to say that "the chief cause of evil is that the towns lack the pleasantness, which is the most important condition of cheerfulness, hopefulness, physical and mental health and strength of all classes, for the poorest as well as for the richest." *

6.—Housing and Morals. What, then, are the direct results of these evils—scarcity of accommodation, high rents, insanitary houses, scant supply of sanitary arrangements, unwholesome surroundings and general dinginess of environment—upon the masses of our working people? Must not the result be a great hindrance to common morality, a general disregard of the decencies and amenities of life? "It is true that their effect (*i.e.* of the evils mentioned) is not all it might be; the natural virtues of working people have a really marvellous power of resistance and recuperation." † Yet we cannot refrain from asking what are the chances of morality existing where members of several families live in one room, or even if single families live in one room tenements with their grown-up sons and daughters? This question is a religious and moral as well as a physical question. The *Daily News* Census, carefully analysed, has proved that apathy and indifference to religion and religious life go hand in hand with poverty and overcrowding. ‡ There is no inducement to men and women

* Cf. "Example of Germany," p. 21.
† Mr. R. C. K. Ensor, *Independent Review*, February, 1906. Cf. Booth, Final Vol., p. 172.
‡ Cf. "The Religious Life of London," p. 27.

in such surroundings to face and overcome the temptations of life, but rather there is everything to render them weak and thus liable to yield to drink, gambling and licentiousness.

The great evil of intemperance is as much an effect as a cause of overcrowding. This the Housing Commission of 1885 cautiously asserted; and it has since been pointed out* that "of the six counties most remarkable for drunkenness in recent years, no less than four, *viz.:* Northumberland, Durham, Pembrokeshire and Cumberland, are remarkable for overcrowding; while the remaining two, *viz.:* Lancashire and Glamorganshire, are also counties which contain a considerable proportion of densely crowded districts."

7.—**Housing and Death Rate.** But it is when we come to the vital statistics of our towns that the most direct results of overcrowding can be seen. The *British Medical Journal* asserts: "It cannot be in accordance with the requirements of civilised life that all the functions of family life should be carried on in a single-roomed dwelling." And this same authority emphasises the fact that the highest death-rate from phthisis† is always found with the largest proportion of overcrowding. But it is not only in the case of this special disease that the death-rate is higher in proportion to the overcrowding. It is an ascertained, and well-nigh universal

* "The Temperance Problem" (Rowntree and Sherwell).

† For a special case in which this was proved in Germany cf. "Example of Germany," p. 187.

fact that the greater the density of population
the higher will be the death-rate from all causes.
Once more we may take our three cities to
illustrate this law; after giving the death-rate
for the three typical areas of the working-class
population in York, Mr. Rowntree summarises
the figures as follows:—"It will then be seen
that the mortality amongst the very poor is more
than twice as high as amongst the best paid
section of the working classes.* It is amongst
the very poor that the most overcrowding is found
and the worst general conditions prevail. In
Manchester the story is the same; Mr. T. R.
Marr remarks: "It will be seen that the districts
with high death-rates are those mainly occupied
by the working-classes, and the districts with low
death-rates are either occupied by well-to-do
people or are only gradually receiving an urban
population."†

Turning to the Metropolis, Dr. Newman,
Medical Officer of Health for Finsbury, in his
1906 Report, gives a table which shows, with
the relentless logic of figures, that in Finsbury the death-rate varies in exact proportion to
the number of rooms in the tenement, the death
rate in one-room tenements being as high as 39,
whilst in four-room tenements and upwards it is
only 6·4 per 1000. But the fact that overcrowding always increases the death-rate is especially
true in the case of Infant Mortality.

* "Poverty," chap. vii.
† Manchester Report, p. 19.

FINSBURY, 1903, 1904, 1905, AND 1906.  DEATH RATES FROM ALL AND CERTAIN CAUSES IN HOUSES OR TENEMENTS OF SEVERAL SIZES.

| Size of Tenement. | Census Population, 1901. 101,463‡ | ALL CAUSES. | | | | PHTHISIS. | | | | RESPIRATORY DISEASE (excluding Phthisis). | | | |
|---|---|---|---|---|---|---|---|---|---|---|---|---|---|
| | | Death rate per 1000. 1903. | Death rate per 1000. 1904. | Death rate per 1000. 1905. | Death rate per 1000. 1906. | Death rate per 1000. 1903. | Death rate per 1000. 1904. | Death rate per 1000. 1905. | Death rate per 1000. 1906. | Death rate per 1000. 1903. | Death rate per 1000. 1904. | Death rate per 1000. 1905. | Death rate per 1000. 1906. |
| One-room tenement .. | 14,516 | 38·9 | 40·6 | 32·7 | 39·0 | 4·5 | 4·5 | 3·5 | 3·4 | 9·3 | 9·8 | 6·4 | 8·3 |
| Two-room tenement .. | 31,482 | 22·6 | 21·9 | 19·5 | 22·5 | 2·8 | 2·2 | 2·1 | 2·3 | 5·3 | 4·9 | 5·2 | 4·8 |
| Three-room tenement .. | 21,280 | 11·7 | 14·7 | 12·3 | 14·8 | 1·2 | 2·3 | 1·3 | 1·4 | 2·4 | 3·4 | 2·8 | 2·9 |
| Four-room tenement and upwards of four rooms.. | 33,185 | 5·6 | 7·5 | 6·6 | 6·4 | 0·63 | 1·2 | 0·81 | 0·93 | 0·84 | 1·4 | 1·4 | 1·2 |
| Institutions * .. .. | 1,000 | 16·0 | 28·0 | 8·0 | 33·0 | 7·0 | 5·0 | .. | 14·0 | 4·0 | 8·0 | 6·0 | 7·0 |
| Deaths not traced † .. | .. | 27·3 | 21·6 | 26·8 | 18·5 | 1·3 | 2·5 | 2·8 | 3·8 | 1·0 | 6·2 | 6·9 | 2·3 |
| The Borough Death Rates | | 19·6 | 21·1 | 18·2 | 20·7 | 2·2 | 2·5 | 2·1 | 2·3 | 3·9 | 4·8 | 4·4 | 4·0 |

* Institutions include Common Lodging Houses, Houseless Poor Asylum, House of Retreat, and other similar Institutions (excluding of course, Hospitals, Infirmaries, etc.).  The population is stated approximately only.

† These are deaths (not death-rates) returned as belonging to Finsbury, in which no address was furnished or the deaths were not traceable at the addresses furnished, or for special reasons the deaths were not visited.

‡ For the purposes of this Table it has been necessary to use the Census Population (1901) for all four of the years included in the Table.  It should not, however, be forgotten that the population is declining, and the Death Rates for each year in this Table are, therefore, approximate only.

A glance at the following table will shew this :—

INFANT MORTALITY IN RELATION TO
HOUSING ACCOMMODATION, FINSBURY, 1905-1906.

| Size of Tenement. | Census Popula-tion, 1901. | Infant Mortality per 1,000 births. | | | | | |
|---|---|---|---|---|---|---|---|
| | | All causes. | | Diarrhœa, and other Zymotic Diseases. | | Prematurity, Immaturity. | |
| | | 1905 | 1906 | 1905 | 1906 | 1905 | 1906 |
| One-room tenement .. | 14,516 | 219 | 211 | 53 | 67 | 30 | 69 |
| Two-room tenement .. | 31,482 | 157 | 178 | 42 | 56 | 26 | 48 |
| Three-room tenement | 21,280 | 141 | 188 | 34 | 43 | 44 | 55 |
| Four-room tenement and upwards of four rooms .. .. .. | 33,185 | 99 | 121 | 19 | 26 | 19 | 52 |
| Institutions and Deaths and Births not traced | 1,000 | 39 | 19 | — | 4 | — | 6 |
| The Borough .. | 101,463 | 148 | 157 | 37 | 45 | 27 | 48 |

Not long since, on the building of new tenements in Clerkenwell it was discovered that the number of deaths of infants was actually 447 per 1,000 in this overcrowded district, as against 149 in other parts of the same parish.* The late Medical Officer of Health for Glasgow, Dr. T. B. Russell, said "Of all children who die in Glasgow before they complete their fifth year, 32 per cent. die in houses of one apartment, and not two per cent. in houses of five apartments and upwards. This may be due to insufficient or improper food, but

* Cf. Mr. Rowntree's figures, chap. viii. " Poverty." " We thus see that in the poorest area one child out of every four dies before it is twelve months old."

it is also to be accounted for by lack of fresh air."

Some towns and districts still allow back-to-back houses, notwithstanding the fact that death-rates of all kinds rise in proportion to the increased percentage of such houses and the narrowness of the streets. There are only a few cities in which new ones are being constructed, but Leeds is yet unconverted as to the evils of this system. The following table * illustrates clearly the ill effect which lack of "through ventilation" has upon the inhabitants of such houses :—

| | Population. | Mortality per 1,000 Population. | | | |
|---|---|---|---|---|---|
| | | All Cases. | Lung Diseases, including Phthisis. | Phthisis. | Principal Zymotic Diseases. |
| Dr. H. Niven (Manchester, 1891-4)— | | | | | |
| Selected Districts, all houses .. .. .. | 75,233 | 30·3 | 8·2 | 2·7 | 4·0 |
| Selected Districts, back-to-back houses | 9,726 | 37·0 | 9·7 | 3·0 | 6·0 |
| Dr. H. Jones (Shipley, 1887-92)— | | | | | |
| Through Houses (Saltaire) .. .. .. | 4,218 | 15·6 | 3·6 | 2·7 | 1·08 |
| Whole District (Shipley) .. .. .. .. | 16,000 | 16·2 | 4·0 | 2·3 | 1·7 |
| Back-to-back in 75 ft. Streets .. .. .. | 2,200 | 18·1 | 4·9 | 2·8 | 1·3 |
| Back-to-back in 45 ft. Streets .. .. .. | 1,245 | 22·5 | 5·7 | 4·1 | 1·8 |
| Back-to-back in 30 ft. Streets .. .. | 710 | 28·1 | 7·4 | 4·6 | 2·9 |
| Back-to-back in Total Streets .. .. | 4,155 | 21·1 | 5·1 | 3·4 | 1·7 |
| Dr. A. Evans (Bradford, 1890-2)— | | | | | |
| Six Wards under 60 per cent. back-to-back .. .. .. .. .. | 202,975 | 19·8 | — | 1·71 | — |
| Nine Wards over 60 per cent. back-to-back .. .. .. .. .. | | 23·7 | — | 1·93 | — |
| Dr. J. Sykes (St. Pancras, 1890-2)— | | | | | |
| Stable Dwellings .. .. .. .. .. | 2,766 | 27·4 | 8·0 | 2·28 | 4·8 |

* "Public Health and Housing," by Dr. J. F. J. Sykes.

**8.—Secondary Effects of Bad Housing.**
Nor is it only to death or actual disease that the
evil of overcrowding is limited. The general
low vitality of those who inhabit overcrowded
dwellings is visibly apparent and takes a heavy
toll of the efficiency of labour in our great cities.
The Royal Commission on Labour expressly stated
that "upon the lowest average every workman or
workwoman lost about twenty days in the year
from simple exhaustion," and that this was largely
to be attributed to the conditions under which
these workpeople live. Dr. John Tatham asserts
that "the vitality of men at 57 in Manchester is
about equal to that of men of 65 in the rest of
England." Why all this terrible, yet preventible
waste of human material, waste of energy, waste
of health, physical and moral, and waste of life
itself? What is it that is wanting? What is the
remedy? It can be put in one word—Home.
That is, a house fulfilling, at least, the minimum
of health requirements and occupied by not more
than the maximum number of persons permitted
by the Public Health Authority—a home where
morality and religion, family life and affection can
develop if the inhabitants be so minded.

# CHAPTER V.

## GENERAL REMEDIES.

---

"Our delicate impalpable sorrows, our keen aching, darling emotions, how strange, almost unreal they seem by the side of the gross mass of filthy misery that clogs the life of great cities!" (ARNOLD TOYNBEE.)

---

IN dealing with the general remedies, proposed by many for the solution of the problem which we have been stating, it is most important to grasp the fact that this housing question is only a part of the still greater and more complex problem of poverty. All the intricate and difficult points arising out of the poverty of the working classes have a distinct bearing on the Housing question. As we have seen, it is inextricably bound up with such diverse matters as the health of the people, the land question, the readjustment of taxation, the growth of pauperism, and immorality.

There is some truth in the saying that we cannot make people good by Acts of Parliament, but it is equally true that we can make them bad by unjust legislation. We may not be able to solve the

housing problem by legislative measures only,
but it is of supreme importance to offer the conditions under which a healthy, moral and decent
life is possible. The true housing reformer, however, will welcome every force working towards
the moral uplift of the people. Such a force, it is
contended, can be exerted by every right-thinking
landlord acting on the lines laid down by Miss
Octavia Hill.

1.—**Miss Octavia Hill's System.** Some
maintain that the whole question of slumdom
is *mainly a question of mismanagement.* There is no
doubt that a great deal of the wilful neglect shown
by the tenants in our slums is induced in the first
place by the neglect of the landlord. A recent
American writer claims that this is certainly so in
the case of the New York tenements. " The
complaint," he says, " was universal among the
tenants that they were entirely uncared for—the
agent's instructions were simple, but emphatic :
collect the rents in advance, or, failing, eject the
occupant." The case is well put by the American
Council of Hygiene, quoted in this book ; " Some
of them," they report, in reference to these slum
owners, " are persons of the highest character, but
they fail to appreciate the responsibility that rests
upon them."* It is towards the cure of this double
neglect—neglect of the tenants by the landlords and
neglect of their homes largely through ignorance
by the tenants—that the energies of Miss Octavia

* " The Peril and the Preservation of the Home,' Jacob A.
Riis.

Hill and her trained band of workers have been directed for a number of years past. It is needless here to describe, in any detail, the methods of work which Miss Hill has initiated; they are now well known, being exemplified by many successful experiments. We may, however, quote a recent testimonial to the value of this enterprise. "Your committee find by experience that improvement of the dwellings does not always result in an improvement of the habits of the tenants; this latter very desirable reform must of necessity be a slower process than the former, and can only be achieved by patient, personal work such as that so successfully accomplished by Miss Octavia Hill and her ladies in London. The Corporation cannot force property owners to adopt such a system, but they can demonstrate its immense advantage to all concerned by giving an object lesson in the management of their own homes."*

It is with the view of improving the habits of the tenants, especially those of the really bad tenants, that Miss Octavia Hill and her helpers work in any slum area of which they can gain possession for this purpose. As one of these workers has expressed it: " The problem, then, is to get hold of the slums and bring the occupants under some sort of effective control. By 'slum' I mean simply neglected, filthy houses and blocks filled with disorderly tenants."† She argues that

* Report of Birmingham Housing Committee, 1906.
† See *Economical Review*, April, 1900, Alice Lewis.

such a "slum" can be converted into a decent, orderly street by proper management of the tenants; that such management needs a strong force behind it, and that there is already present in the situation such a force, *viz.* the landlord. " The power of the landlord for good or evil is practically unique," she affirms, and pleads that this power may be used, as it has not been used very largely before, for the good of the tenants. Hence the regular house-to-house visits of such workers, visits which not only serve to collect the weekly rents, but have the express object of ascertaining the individual conditions of each tenant, of encouraging the improvement of these conditions, and of giving such counsel and advice as may be required from time to time. The remedy has just this to recommend it—that it works from within outwards and has not to be superimposed, as it were, from the top. It is a remedy which seeks to create a healthy opinion on housing matters where it is the most needed, *viz.* at the foundation of the social structure, the homes of the people themselves.*

2.—The Great Need—A Sound Public Opinion. No administrative or legislative remedy can be effective apart from the formation of a sound public opinion. It is for the Christian Churches especially to throw the whole weight

* Cf. a Paper, by Miss O. Hill, reprinted from the *Daily Chronicle*, in Birmingham Report (p. 113). Some Building Societies work now on these principles of tenant-management, *e.g.* the *Glasgow Working Men's Dwellings Co.*, the *Peabody Trust*, etc.

of their influence on the side of reform in this question of housing. Each church, settlement, mission hall should be a centre of light, uplift and moral healing—a place where all the forces which make for a better life may act and react upon the people. Again, the importance of our elementary schools in this connection can hardly be exaggerated. The children should be taught what are the proper conditions of a good and healthy life as a distinct part of their educational curriculum. They should be physically so trained that healthy bodies will develop healthy minds, thus predisposed to good rather than to evil. They should be instructed in the value of pure air, adequate exercise, and personal cleanliness. Quite recently two proposals have been made which point in the right direction; firstly, the provision of compulsory medical inspection in our elementary schools; secondly, the recommendation of Dr. James Kerr, Medical Officer to the Education Committee of the London County Council, in respect of systematic bathing of the scholars at these schools.* Both these proposals, and many more of the same sort, must be boldly carried out, along with a vigorous crusade against juvenile smoking, juvenile gambling and kindred evils. This is the kind of educational influence

---

* For twenty years this has been quite a common custom in the elementary schools of Germany, and has resulted in undoubted improvement in the hygiene of the scholars. See Report to L.C.C. by Drs. J. Kerr and F. Rose on " Bathing Arrangements in Schools in Germany and Holland " (July. 1906).

that must proceed from our elementary schools, an influence that should be maintained and strengthened in the various Sunday schools. It seems quite time for the Sunday school to revise its methods if it is to continue to be the great moral force in the future that it has been in the past. Such good training, begun at school, must be continued, during the critical years of youth, by evening classes, social clubs and like helpful influences.

Efforts like these have been made, and are being made to improve the social life of our people. What is wanted is more systematic effort and more devoted energy to further such effort.

3.—**Constructive Philanthropy.** A good deal of the disheartening apathy observable in these matters is due to absolute ignorance. Hence the great value of such organisations as the Liverpool Housing Association, the Bradford and Halifax and Sheffield City Guilds of Help, the Citizens' Associations of Manchester and Salford and York. These organisations help to keep alive the enthusiasm, and also to disseminate true knowledge of the evil conditions still prevalent in our country, and the proper cure of those evils. The feeling of the working classes has never been sufficiently roused to the great importance of healthy homes with adequate accommodation. When this feeling has been properly awakened, we may expect the local authorities to bestir themselves. Until then we shall have to encounter apathy, neglect, and even open opposition to all reform. "It is literally true," says a recent writer, "that hundreds of British local authorities are, to a large extent, neglecting their health and sanitary duties, as witness for example, the inaction of most of them in regard to Part II. of the Housing Act. The duty of condemning insanitary houses under Sec. 32 of this part of the Housing Act is made perfectly clear and definite, yet many councils act as if it were optional and not a matter of duty at all."* It is to the interest of all that the workers of our people should be better housed, but most of all to the interest of the workers themselves. It is the working class, with its great majority in numbers, that must rouse itself on this question. Its influence, rightly exerted, would outweigh all other policies or parties. The local authority could do infinitely more than it does at present without any fresh enactments, but the driving force, the dynamic, is lacking.

4.—Public Health Committees (Voluntary). It has been suggested that voluntary committees should be formed, with the express purpose of seeing that the existing housing legislation is carried out. Committees of this sort, but appointed by statute, were formed in Belgium in 1889, and have been of considerable service in this direction, and a recent Housing Act in Holland has established "local boards of health." . . . "They have no administrative power at all, and herein

* *Municipal Journal*, August 31st, 1906. H. R. Aldridge.

F

rests their special interest. Their work is supplementary to that of the Town and District Councils, and they do not relieve these authorities of any responsibility. The task entrusted to them is that of stimulating municipal housing and sanitary action, and, if necessary, of criticising those local authorities guilty of neglect in regard to health matters."* Working men should form some such Voluntary Public Health and Housing Committees,† and press for a house-to-house inspection of all the insanitary and overcrowded districts. A Local Government Board circular of June 22nd, 1900, points out that this is the duty of the local authority.‡ Again, wherever there is an insufficient supply of workmen's houses a deputation of working men should approach the local authority, and urge that Part III. of the Housing Act be put into operation. Above all, a vigilant watch by the public must be kept on all local administration. Dishonest dealing and corruption on a public body generally begin with such important matters as the public health or the housing of the people. It is as difficult for the slum-owner to see defects in his own property as it is for the speculating builder to be quite disinterested in building schemes, and the risk of mismanagement of public affairs by such persons must not be run by our Town and

* *Municipal Journal*, August 31st, 1906.

† Similar committees have already been formed in various towns by the Friends' Social Union, the Christian Social Union, and the Wesleyan Methodist Social Guild.

‡ Cf. § 92 Public Health Act, and § 32 of the Housing Act.

District Councils. Much good, honest work is being done by many of these councils. Let public opinion see to it that this high standard is maintained.

5.—Slum Clearances. But we must pass on to discuss another general remedy which has often, especially at the beginning of reform in housing matters, been advocated, *viz.* the rigid suppression' of slum areas. It has frequently been argued— " If these fearful conditions prevail in these slum areas why not make a clean sweep of evils and slums alike? If the slums are the plague spots; abolish them." For the clearance of such large insanitary areas it is necessary to use Part I., as we have seen, of the Housing of the Working Classes Act. The London County Council has had eight such schemes, involving the clearance of 31¾ acres at a cost of £1,045,000. One of the most notable of such schemes, and, in fact, by far the most extensive, was the Boundary Street (Bethnal Green) area.

6.—The Boundary Street Scheme. Fifteen acres of slums were cleared at a cost of £280,000 between the years 1893 and 1897; and this clearance affected a population of 5,719 inhabitants who were thereby temporarily displaced. Of this population no less than 2,118 lived in 752 single-roomed tenements, and the death rate of this terribly insanitary area was over 40 per 1,000, in contrast to about 18 per 1,000 for London generally! In 1900 the new buildings, with streets laid out on radial lines, were opened by the Prince of Wales,

and in place of the slums there were found well
planned roads, fifty feet in width, planted with
trees, leading to an open space, and tenements of
one to six rooms, capable of accommodating 5,524
persons, so constructed as to secure the maximum
light and air space with the minimum of discomfort. There are also baths, a laundry and one
or two club-rooms on the premises; the average
weekly rent per room is about 2s. 10d. The
general death rate and the infant mortality have
been reduced by about 50 per cent.

Somewhat similar schemes, though on a much
smaller scale, have been carried out by the London
County Council in Clare Market (Strand) and in
St. Pancras; also by other cities, such as Manchester, Leeds, Birmingham and Edinburgh.

7.—**Disadvantages of Slum Clearance
Schemes.** Now, though there can be no question
that these schemes have certainly benefited the
areas which they have affected—the reduction of
the death rate in the case of the Bethnal Green
area is sufficient proof of this—yet there are many
arguments which may be used against this somewhat obvious remedy of our housing evils. The
first of these objections is the almost prohibitive
cost of large improvement schemes of this sort.
Only such a large body as the London County
Council could undertake successfully a scheme
like the Boundary Street area. Even so,
the expense has been enormous, owing to the
huge price paid for the land, compensation to
the slum owners, and high working expenses.

About £32,000 per acre has been paid on the average for the land alone. The clearing of the Bethnal Green area cost considerably more than a quarter of a million pounds, besides the cost of the building, which was another quarter of a million. This latter sum will, of course, be gradually repaid by the rents, but the former was charged to the rates. Such enormous cost, in most cases, precludes any clearance of large slum areas, and, even when such clearances are decided upon, causes much discussion, dispute and consequent delay.

But another objection to the clearance of slum areas is that, though the areas cleared are immensely improved the general result is the driving of the slum dwellers into other quarters of the same town and the possible creation of a new slum. It is a well-known fact that when slums have been replaced by good, healthy dwellings the new population is quite other than that which inhabited the area before. In the case of the Boundary Street clearance it was estimated that not 5 per cent. of the original people returned to occupy the new quarters supplied. One reason for this was that such very poor people could not afford to pay the high rents which the new building scheme was bound to entail. It is also true to some extent that such tenants do not really desire better accommodation ; they are, and have always been, slum dwellers and prefer to remain so. As one report of an investigator in Mr. Charles Booth's work says, " They don't want such (*i.e.* new) accommodation, and would not take it if offered, and, if they did, it would only end in the new buildings being spoiled."* Thus it is that the legal provisions which exist for re-housing tenants displaced by building schemes (especially in connection with railway extension, etc.) are largely ineffective. Most of the slum dwellers very much dislike having their dwellings, miserably unhealthy and overcrowded as they may be, interfered with; and this is also a serious bar to rebuilding schemes. Still, we have to remember, after this objection has been given its full force, that in such schemes, whatever benefits any one section of the working classes, is likely to have an indirect effect upon all other grades.

Yet another objection to such clearances is the high value which they indirectly set upon other insanitary areas. As we have seen, most of the displaced slum dwellers remove to other slums, thus forcing the already too high rents up to a higher figure still. These fresh accessions to already overcrowded districts increase the value of this property to the owners, and the purchase price (especially the compensation price in the case of compulsory purchase) rises in proportion. This method of dealing with our slums "has encouraged the development of a new industry, *viz.* the buying up of property in insanitary areas in order to reap a rich harvest of compensation from the municipal pocket."†

* Final Vol. p. 175.  † "Housing Handbook," p. 8.

The truth is that the slum dwelling is a malignant social disease and its poisonous roots lie deeper than is generally recognised in the body politic. We cannot cure this disease by merely removing some of its deadly plague-spots. The cure, if cure there be, must be altogether more comprehensive, wider in its scope and broader in its application.

8.—**Housing in the Suburbs.** This brings us to a general remedy which is of far greater importance because more effective, *viz.* the construction of more new houses, together possibly with the reconstruction of old ones, so as to accommodate a larger number of inhabitants. Many have argued that private enterprise, following the law of demand and supply, will do all that is required in this direction. In some cases, it has fully met the need for additional accommodation, especially in response to a demand made effective by ability to pay a high rent. But what has been the result of this activity in a large number of instances ? On the one hand, simply the erection of new *suburban* slums or such rows of badly built, ill-planned houses as must become slums in a very few years' time; and, on the other hand, the conversion of old houses without necessary sanitary appliances and proper adaptation, into tenements for many families, thus intensifying the already existing evil. The *laissez-faire* doctrine, which the advocates of private enterprise favour, has frequently handed our cities over to the jerry-builder and the poorer tenants to the house

speculator and slum owner.   A great deal more
care must be taken in the future as to how and
where these houses are to be built ; and it cannot
be too often pointed out that private enterprise
breaks down just where the need is greatest.

9.—The Art of City Making.   This brings
us face to face with the whole question of town
development, a problem of the utmost importance
to all interested in Housing Reform.   " In a dim
sort of way many persons understand that the
time has come when art and skill and foresight
should control what so far has been left to chance
to work out; that there should be a more orderly
conception of civic action ; that there is a real art
of city-making, and that it behoves this generation
to master and practise it." *   This " art of city-
making," *viz.* of the proper planning and development of each large town by a representative
council of its citizens, is an art which flourishes
much more in Germany and even in America
than it does in our own country.   Prof. Geddes,
whose useful work in this direction is now well-
known, reluctantly admits this.   He says: " But
though *our* cities are still as a whole planless,
their growth as yet little better than a mere casual
accretion and agglomeration, if not a spreading
blight, American and German cities are now
increasingly affording examples of comprehensive
design of extension and of internal improvement."†

---

*See the *Times* for July 20th, 1904 (leading article).

† See an interesting paper read by Prof. Geddes before the
Sociological Society in " Sociological Papers, 1904."

This opinion is in entire agreement with that of Mr. T. C. Horsfall, the acknowledged authority on this matter as regards Germany.* He points out how the growth of our towns must be definitely planned as in Germany, the most notable illustration being Frankfurt, where streets are built to get the maximum of sunlight, and sufficient land is set aside for open spaces. Our Town Councils, in many instances, are quite careless in this respect, and fail to utilise even those powers which present legislation gives them.

The importance of the proper development of our large towns is seen when we realise how rapidly our suburbs are growing. The urgency of this part of the Housing Problem cannot be questioned, for every day sees in each city fresh developments, and it is all important whether this development be careless and haphazard, or along properly planned and well regulated lines.

As an illustration of this let us take a large suburban area in Greater London. " West Ham has been built in thirty years; East Ham is now plastered beyond it, each with their hundreds of thousands of inhabitants. . . . All this is of the folly that declines to look ahead. Thirty years ago, at little expense and no discomfort, a broad ring, half a mile wide, of park and play-ground could have been driven round London with building developed only on the further side. What a different future would await tens of thousands of

‡ Cf. "Example of Germany," especially pp. 26-9, 63-7, and 160-72.

the growing children of the city to-day had such a beneficent work been accomplished. Every day that passes removes some promise of possibility."*

Every thousand pounds spent in preventing the growth of slums in the outskirts of a city would be of more value than ten times that amount spent on slum clearance at its centre. The Housing Problem is to be solved by the formation of suitable and healthy suburbs, which can be easily reached from the heart of the city, rather than by the abolition of slum areas, or even the construction of model dwellings, within the inner ring of the city. This prevention, which is better than cure, will necessitate new adminstrative machinery to deal with it; and this machinery must be created soon or it will be too late in the case of London and many other of our large towns. The whole of the district round each large town should be placed, for administrative purposes, under some one central authority. This is especially true of London, for the forty different local authorities, whose spheres of jurisdiction adjoin the London County Council area, cannot act with that unanimity of purpose which is necessary in such an important matter. Some such central authority is needed if the districts surrounding the London of the County Council are not to be lost for ever to the jerry-builder and slum-maker.

This authority, in most towns the municipality, must have large powers of land purchase outside

---

* Cf. " Towards a Social Policy," chap. ix.

its own immediate area. It should be able to obtain possession of such land "*against future needs*" at a reasonable rate, so that development may be along the lines of a definite policy of enlargement and improvement. Such German towns as Dusseldorf, Ulm and Cöln have used their powers in this direction to the permanent benefit of the city. They have procured the best surveyors and architects and planned the future development of the city on the most approved lines. This is where our own Port Sunlight, Bournville and "Garden City" have pioneered the way in the matter of town planning. All our large cities must, sooner or later, follow their example.

The authority with this additional power must go on to erect suitable dwellings in these properly. planned suburbs. Whether this be done by the authority itself, or delegated to private enterprise, * such regulations must be imposed and insisted upon as shall insure a sufficient supply of healthy, home-like houses. As Sir Thomas Barclay has said : " A beautiful city is an investment for health, intellect, imagination. Genius all the world over is associated, wherever it has been connected with cities, with beautiful cities. To grow up among things of beauty ennobles the population." To this matter we shall have to return when we deal with the subject of Garden Cities and Garden Suburbs.

* Cf. the Building Societies of Public Utility in Germany.

# CHAPTER VI.

## THE LAND QUESTION AND TAXATION REFORM.

"Back to the land! It is the storehouse of wealth; Nature's universal bank—a bank that never breaks and never dwindles, that honours every draft when drawn by labour's hand. It is a moral, a physical, a political, a national regeneration." (ERNEST JONES.)

IN memorable words Ruskin has described the proper possession of the land by the people as their greatest inheritance. "Land," he says, "carefully tended by the hand of man, so far as to remove from it unsightlinesses and evidences of decay, guarded from violence, and inhabited, under man's affectionate protection, by every kind of living creature that can occupy it in peace, is the most precious 'property' that human beings can possess."*

This "property," which is invaluable for the well-being of the people is, however, largely a monopoly in England to-day. The fact, already referred to, that four-fifths of the whole of the land in this country is in the hands of a few thousand landowners should be sufficient testimony to the truth of this statement.

* "Munera Pulveris," § 16.

Moreover, since our land is possessed by the few, and it appears to be increasingly difficult to largely extend its ownership, it acquires an unnatural and abnormal value. This *dearness* of land has many ill effects on housing in our cities and towns.

1.—The "Towniness of Towns." It has been responsible for that evil of our large cities which has been described in the general term, " the towniness of towns," *i.e.* the lack of open spaces, the narrow streets and few gardens which give the general air of dinginess to these centres of population. Where urban land is in the possession of a few great land-owners who practically own some of our cities and who, in many cases, deliberately keep back much of the unused land for the rise in value which is certain to come—only the minimum amount possible will be purchased for housing purposes. It is obvious how direct must be the connection between this dearness of land and such evils as overcrowding, lack of open space and general insanitary conditions of living.

2.—The House Famine. But another ill effect which this artificial value of land has upon our cities is its creation of that house famine of which we have already spoken. We have seen that private enterprise has very largely failed to supply a sufficient quantity of dwelling-houses for the working classes. One of the main reasons for this is that, in consequence of the high price of land, buildings cannot be put up at a rent which it would be possible for the workers, who need such houses, to pay, and which would at the same time make a safe investment for the builder. It has been pointed out that this is so even in the case of building enterprise not strictly "private." "This 'corner' in land has operated very injuriously on those semi-public, semi-philanthropic bodies such as artisans' dwellings' companies and co-operative societies, that have been endeavouring to cope with the deficiency in the supply of good houses. So much has their work been hampered by this and other causes, that the great public companies and trusts, after building over 30,000 dwellings have practically suspended operations during the last ten years, in spite of the average return of four and a half per cent which they get on their capital."*

3.—The Land Monopoly. Yet another effect of this dearness of land—an effect which vitally concerns our housing question—is the direct encouragement that it gives to that rural exodus with which we have already dealt. The fact that our land is largely in the hands of the few great landowners hinders that free access to it which is so necessary a feature of a prosperous agricultural people. The depopulation of the country might at least be checked were it possible for the labourer to maintain himself in independence. A proof of this fact is the remarkable success of small holdings where they have been tried on a fairly liberal scale. Authorities on this question,

*See " Housing Handbook," p. 10.

such as Lord Carrington, Mr. R. Winfrey, M.P., and Mr. Rider Haggard express the utmost confidence in the success of any system of small holdings where it can be tried over a sufficiently large area and worked on a moderately liberal plan. *

It is not so much true that the people "have been drawn to the towns like moths to the flame," † as that they have been driven out of our rural districts by the difficulty of obtaining land, the scarcity of employment, and, so we must add, by insufficiency of house accommodation. One of the first remedies, then, for the housing evils of which we have been speaking would be a cheapening of land, and the letting of such land in holdings of a convenient size. How this may be done it is scarcely our province to discuss here, but what we have to say in the rest of this chapter will have some bearing on the question. But by some means or other there must be freer access to the land if there is to be a lessening of the evil of overcrowding in our cities. The Select Committee of the House of Commons to consider the " Housing

---

* Cf. an interesting pamphlet, " The Small Holdings of "England," by L. Jebb. Co-operative Small Holdings Society. (6d.)

† Cf. statement by Mr. Chas. Trevelyan, M.P. : " It is not that the glare of shops is preferred by all men to the sunset ; that the quieter glories of springtime and haymaking and gardening cannot compensate for the music-hall and the lure of the crowded city. The same kind of men from town and country settle down happily in Canada and New Zealand on the land. But in England the land is closed to them." See ' *Land Taxation and the Use of Land.*' " Coming Men on Coming Questions," Pamphlet XX.

of the Working Classes Acts Amendment Bill,
1906," makes some interesting recommendations
in this direction.*

4.—**Municipal Ownership of Land.**   This
power to purchase land is most urgent, and
especially so in the case of the municipalities.
Our municipalities must have greatly increased
powers of land purchase around their borders,
if our towns and cities are to be rightly developed
in the immediate future.   Germany is far ahead
of us in this respect; and the reason for this is
that the land monopoly, of which we have been
speaking, is largely unknown in that country.
" The purchase by German towns of land outside
their boundaries is rendered easier than the
purchase of land would be for English towns,
even if they were as free from legal restrictions
as German towns are, by the fact that land is
in far more hands in Germany than in England,
and holders of small quantities of land are, as a
rule, less able to hold their land till it will sell for
a very high price than are the holders of large
estates."†   Mr. Horsfall instances the loss to the
township of Manchester of Trafford Park, which
would have formed a valuable suburb for the
people, the Council having failed‡ to previously

* See Chapter on Rural Housing, page 44.

† " The Example of Germany," by T. C. Horsfall, pp.
82 and 18.

‡ Cf. also a similar instance in regard to Sheffield mentioned in *Municipal Journal* for November 16th, 1906.   In
this case the difficulty seems to be " in the inelastic nature
of the regulations under which the department (the L.G.B.)
acts."

adopt a comprehensive policy which would have
insured the purchase of this desirable property as
a permanent investment for the city.

There must be real reform in this direction in
the case of all our cities, reform that shall give
them large powers to acquire land without having
to pay those swollen rates for compensation which
are the difficulty of many municipalities to-day.
We must have also a considerable simplification of
procedure in land conveyance if any movement in
this direction is to be permanently useful. This
achieved, the growth of population would mean
the lowering of the death rate, and the increase of
municipal wealth. The good results of such a wise
policy of land purchase would be many. The
suburban slum would be a thing impossible in the
future. Town development would take place
along properly planned lines. Good and sufficient
building, either by private enterprise, or by the
municipality would result. And, last but not least,
the increased value of the land would go into the
municipal exchequer and thus relieve the rates,
which, at the present time, are such an incubus
upon the proper development of the city.

5.—Taxation Reform. This latter consideration leads us on to the important question of
taxation reform. The Report of the Royal Commission on Housing, already mentioned, contains
the following significant words : "Your Majesty's
Commissioners must observe with reference to . . .
nearly every proposal for improving the dwellings
of the working classes . . . that the present

G

incidence of local taxation stands seriously in the way of all progress and reform." As we have already seen, the fact that rent consumes from a quarter to one-third of the worker's wage in England to-day, makes it impossible for good accommodation to be secured by any but the best paid workers. The rest have to be content with poor accommodation at a rent which inflicts hardships in many respects. Now one of the chief factors in this high rent charge, a factor which of course helps to determine the amount of the rent, is the increasing charge of the rates imposed by local taxation. There is almost a universal outcry against this increase in rates, an increase which shows no signs of abatement. Anything from 20% to even 40% of the total rent has now to be paid in rates to the local authorities of any of our large towns. Nearly all seem agreed that some relief must be forthcoming, for this is a burden which seems to press heaviest on those who are least able to bear it, and who are ignorant that they really do bear it, *viz.* the poorer classes who, for one reason or another, are often obliged to live near the heart of the town. Lately a comparison has been drawn between the condition of the working classes in the old food-tax days and their condition in the present house-tax days. There have not been wanting those who maintain that the state of affairs is not much better now than it was then, that only the point of incidence of taxation has been changed. If, so these persons argue, *food* has been immensely cheapened by free trade, why not attempt to apply

the same principles of free trade to the *houses* of
the people, for the dwelling-place is as certain a
necessity of life as bread or meat ? It is at this
point that taxation reformers and housing reformers
meet to offer their suggestions of reform. Putting
it as briefly as possible these suggestions are three
in number :—

(1) To tax what is known as the " unearned
increment" whenever urban property is sold or
re-leased.*

(2) That a tax be levied by the State on all sites
as distinguished from buildings or other improvements on those sites, and

(3) As an alternative and improvement on this
second suggestion, that this tax on site-values
should be levied not by the State, but locally, *i.e.*
should form a new system of *rating*.

6.—Rating of Site Values. Inasmuch as this
last proposal is, as we have said, an improvement
on the second and also includes the advantages of
the first without its disadvantages, we shall confine
ourselves to briefly discussing this one only, *viz.*
the rating of site values. This suggested reform,
largely urged now by men of every shade of
opinion, and especially advocated by the progressive
members of the London County Council, is usually
backed by the following arguments :—

(i.) Though there is, in some agricultural
districts of England, an undoubted *de*crement in
the value of land, yet, on the whole, land values

* Cf. an able article, by A. Hook, advocating the suggestion, in the *Economic Review* of October, 1906.

have increased and are still steadily increasing. In all large towns this increase of value has been so remarkable that the phenomenon of "the unearned increment" is now known and discussed by all interested in social matters. This increase of value, so familiar to all readers that it will be unnecessary here to give any examples in illustration of it, has been almost entirely created by the presence and exertion of the community as a whole rather than by the individual landowner, a fact which has led both taxing and housing reformers to ask why this increment should not be available for local taxation. It is the locality that has created the increased value, why then should not the locality reap some return in the form of rates from such values ? Thus Professor Marshall, one of our leading political economists, says : "There may be great difficulty in allocating the betterments due to any particular improvement. But, as it is . . . much of the rates raised on building values for public improvements, is really a free gift of wealth to owners who are already fortunate."* And he goes on to suggest that some form of taxation of these betterments is not only just but expedient. This unearned increment would be effectually taxed if the incidence of the rates fell not, as it does now, on buildings and improvements on the site, but on the site separately. All sites would thus have to be separately valued, not on the present basis (which is often below

* Cf. Parliamentary Paper, C 9528 of 1899.

the true value of the site) but at that amount
which a willing buyer would give to a reasonable
vendor.  We will return shortly to the question
as to whether this valuation is feasible.  It is
only important here to notice that there are two
distinct parts to this proposal to tax land values;
first the separate valuation of sites, and, second,
rating on that separate valuation.

7.—Vacant  Land  and  Void  Houses.
(ii.) Another argument, brought forward on behalf
of the rating of site values, is that vacant land and
void houses which have so long escaped their fair
share of the burden of local taxation would, by
this system, be put under proper contribution to
the rates.  The system of rating urban land now
in use not only falls most heavily on the occupier
of buildings on that land, but actually induces
landowners to keep land vacant for the rising
value which is certain to come through the
nearness of the city.  This, of course, forces up
the rent of the land already used for building, and
thus helps to cause the existing house famine.
The effect of rating such vacant land would be, of
course, to bring it into the market, whilst the rate
on vacant houses would tend to fill such houses
with tenants at reduced rents?and thus to lower
rents generally.  If the question of the right of
the community to heavily tax "the unearned
increment" be still a debateable one, this question
of taxing vacant land can hardly be called so.  It
has been estimated that if such land were rated
as other property, for example, in Halifax, the

city rates would be lessened by 1s. 6d. in the pound. Out of an area of 10,776 acres which the city of Bradford occupies, it is said that no less than 4,512 acres are held back from sale for the rise in value which is certain to come.* There can be no doubt but that a proper rating of vacant land and empty houses would give a real stimulus to private enterprise in building. This activity would have to be carefully watched so as to guard our suburbs from the land speculator and jerry-builder, yet it can hardly be questioned but that such increased building would tend to simplify the problem.

8.—Lowering of Rents. (iii.) Yet another argument which may be adduced in favour of the rating of site values, is that in consequence of urban land coming more freely into the market and building enterprise being stimulated, rent would be materially relieved; and this relief would come where rent is now at its maximum, i.e. in our large industrial centres. As we have seen, it is just here where rent presses most severely on our poorest classes, and any relief of this pressure would have a salutary effect, especially in the direction of slum clearances. Every opportunity given to the freer growth of the city in the suburbs will tend to reduce this congestion at the centre. Abolition of restrictions in the matter of the housing of the people will have the same effect as in the matter of the

* " The Housing Problem in the Towns." C. M. Knowles, " Eighty Club" Pamphlet, p. 31.

people's food, *viz.* increased distribution of supply at a lower price. "Overcrowding," as Sir Henry Campbell-Bannerman recently observed, "is to a large extent due to the maintenance of the same sort of restrictions and privileges at home as Free Trade has abolished for international commerce. The taxation of land values will put an end to the immunity of the landlord enriched by the exertions of others, to the circumscribing of natural expansion."* It is this "natural expansion" which is the all-important matter in the question of housing our workers. It is this, and this alone, that will materially lessen the heavy charge of rent; and so the rating of land values is a proposal to be commended because, by aiding natural expansion, it will tend thus to reduce rents.

9.—**Readjustment of Rate Burden.** (iv.) The last argument to be brought forward in favour of the taxing of site-values is—that such an incidence of local taxation would ensure a fairer sharing of the burden of the rates between owner and occupier. It is a well-known maxim of the economist that the owner really bears the burden of the rates and taxes in that he receives a lower rent than he would otherwise do were the occupier not liable for these burdens. This, however, like many other general maxims, is only partly true. It will be seen how little true it would be when, for example, a long lease is signed by an occupier

* Quoted by Sir F. A. Channing, M.P., in *Independent Review*, for October, 1906.

knowing much less of the neighbourhood, in which he is about to dwell, than the owner, who naturally has an extensive acquaintance with the conditions of house property in that neighbourhood. The occupier, in this case, will not be able to fairly estimate what the rise in rates will be over the long period of his lease; and so superior is the position of the ordinary landlord to that of the tenant, that this attempt to estimate in the rent the burden of the rates, will be more or less, as it is often called, a " blind bargain." It is true that the tenant receives the temporary benefit of the improvements for which the rates are levied, but, when his lease expires, many of these improvements will be entirely in the hands of the owner; and, for these, as far as the tenant is concerned, *i.e.* if he does not renew the lease, the owner will have paid nothing. Even if the lease be renewed and the tenant attempt to get the rent lowered in consequence of such improvements, it will be very difficult for the occupier to get the owner to share the burden equitably, for there is much truth in the statement that a tax tends to stick where it is levied.

This point of the sharing of the rates as between owner and occupier is quite incidental to the main question of the rating of site values and not essential as many seem still to suppose. Yet it is an important additional argument for this new system of rating. At present the occupier certainly bears the heavier share of the burden, and, if a properly regulated and carefully modulated system were introduced by which this burden should be equitably shared, great relief in the increasingly serious pressure of local taxation would be experienced. The actual proposal in this connection by most reformers is that, at any rate at first, half the site rate should be paid by the owner and half by the occupier. The latter would still continue to actually pay the rate, but he would be entitled, as at present in the case of the house tax, to deduct half the amount when paying his rent to the owner. All existing contracts would be considered still binding (which removes one of the chief arguments originally used against the proposal), but at the end of present leases owners would be required to allow half the value of the site rates which occupiers had paid since the new system became law.

**10.—Is Site Valuation Practicable?** In closing this chapter it only remains to ask two simple questions, which can be very briefly answered. Is this valuation of sites practicable? and, What has been already done on behalf of this proposal for the separate rating of sites? In answer to the first question we may mention the opinion, for example, of Mr. Harper, Statistical Officer to the London County Council and a well-known authority on such matters. He maintains that all sites could be separately valued in London for, say, £40,000, and that such a valuation is eminently desirable. We may point to the many German towns and provinces (over seventy), to five out of the seven of our Australian

Governments, to New Zealand,* and most recent
of all to New York—where, in each of these cases,
this valuation is a matter of history, and where
improved systems of taxation have followed on
such valuations.

11.—**The Minority Report of 1901.**   To
answer our final question as to what has been done
in this matter in England, we would first draw
attention to the most important Minority Report
furnished by five out of the fifteen Royal Commissioners on Local Taxation in 1901.   This
Report, signed by the Chairman of the Commission, Lord Balfour of Burleigh, contains the
following recommendations :—

(1) *Site* should be *separately valued from structure.*
(2) Site can bear heavier taxation than structure,
    but all existing contracts must be rigidly
    respected.
(3) There should be a *special site value rate.*
(4) This should be charged also on (*a*) *unoccupied
    property,* and (*b*) on *uncovered land.*

The general conclusion of that report was that
this proposal to rate site values "would do something towards lightening the burdens in respect of
building, and thus something towards solving the
difficult and urgent housing problem."† This
report only followed in the steps of the Royal
Commissioners on Housing who, as far back as

* Cf. Blue Book on Australasia (1906), Cd. 3191.   Price
5d.

† "The Rating of Land Values."   A. W. Fox, C.B.,
Secretary to Royal Commission, pp. 97-115.

1885, recommended taxing " land available for building " outside our towns at 4% on its selling value.

It is a significant fact that in 1904 and, again, in 1905 such a Bill was passed, on the second reading, by a majority of no less than 67 and 90 votes respectively in a Conservative House of Commons. No less than two hundred of our leading municipalities have declared in favour of such a rating reform. In fact, the London County Council have had a definite scheme on this question for some years past; this scheme recommends a separate valuation of each site, this valuation to be the basis of a special " owner's tax " to be limited by Parliament to a minimum of 6d. in the £. It has been pointed out that the London County Council has already practically taxed site values by its " Tower Bridge Southern Approach " Act (1895), when it imposed a " Betterment Charge " of 3% on the site values surrounding the improvement. " If an owner was not satisfied with the County Council's estimate of the final value, he could resort to arbitration, or else could give notice to the County Council to buy it at their own figure "*—an arrangement which would answer some further objections to this proposed rating of site values.

But we have said enough, we hope, to show that this reform is new neither in idea nor in practice. That it may need the separate organization of some

---

* Cf. " Local Taxation in London," chap. iii. M. E. Lange (1906).

central body to administer this reform, and that
some difficulties in valuation and collection may
have to be encountered are questions of debate ;
but that a new source of useful revenue to the
municipality will be created can hardly be doubted,
and this without increasing the burden of the
already over-burdened householder. Such a new
revenue must, of course, be used for further
lessening the evils of town and city life. " We
must never lose sight of the fact that the primary
object of taxing or rating site values in or about
towns is to make our towns habitable."*

That is why we have dealt with it rather fully
here—as being one of the most needed reforms
for the betterment of our cities. " It is not a
mere question of the incidence of rates ; it will
lighten the burden of rents, diminish the evils of
crowding, and relieve the pressure on manufactures."†

* See *Independent Review* : " Measures to accompany Land
Taxation," by F. W. Pethick Lawrence, October, 1906.

† Sir F. A. Channing, M.P., *Independent Review*, October,
1906.

# CHAPTER VII.

## MODEL DWELLINGS AND MUNICIPAL HOUSING.

*" It is only by providing homes for the working people, that is by providing for them not only shelter, but shelter of such kind as to protect life and health and to make family life possible, free from surroundings which tend to immorality, that the evils of crowded city life can be mitigated and overcome."* (*Report of Tenement House Commission.* New York.)

WE have now come to the point when we must briefly review the various kinds of actual buildings which our workers inhabit. This will lead us on to consider the agencies which have erected these buildings and the question of municipal housing.

Six types of buildings have been noted as practically exhausting the housing accommodation open to the worker who does not rank himself as either a pauper or a casual.

1.—The Common Lodging House. Those who have any acquaintance with this sort of residence in any of our large or even small towns, will know that, when in the hands of ordinary lodging-house keepers, it is not a very desirable abode for respectable people, however poor they may be. There is a great lack of cleanliness in such places (notwithstanding regular sanitary inspection), a good deal of rough and bad company, and very few, if any, of those influences which we can associate with the word "home." It is not surprising, therefore, that religious bodies and philanthropists have turned their attention to this kind of accommodation for our poorer people and that we have The Salvation Army Night Shelters, the Church Army Labour Homes and the Rowton lodging-houses for single men. Many municipalities, too, have now built model lodging-houses, notably the London County Council, Glasgow, which has seven such houses, and Manchester. In all such improvements on the common lodging-house of private enterprise, the inmates receive a clean bed (at some of the houses, in separate cubicles), a hot or cold bath, and food from the kitchen at the lowest possible charges.

It will at once be seen that this sort of accommodation only serves a small class of our workers, and, in fact, is open to two objections when supplied on the "model" system; first, that such buildings are costly to build and more costly to maintain, and, secondly, that it is perhaps an unwise thing to make these houses too comfortable, as it may increase the temptation to men to live in such places when they ought to be living in homes of their own, or causing men sometimes even to desert their own wretched homes. It only remains to add that there are in London, Glasgow, Huddersfield and other towns, special lodging houses for women, and that the improvement of accommodation in this case on that provided by "private" lodging house keepers is not only a question of comfort and sanitation but also of morals.

2.—**The Municipal Family Home.** The next type of housing accommodation need detain us only a moment. It is that of the *Municipal Family Home* which has been tried at Glasgow. This experiment was made in order to assist widows or widowers with children who were of necessity compelled by their work to leave the children during the day. It is now used entirely for. widowers and their children, and contains 150 small rooms with dining-room, recreation room, kitchen and crêche. The cost of the building and land was £17,000, or about £106 per head. It is heated with hot water, and lighted with electricity. The charge is a comparatively small one:—

Widower and 1 child ... 4s. 2d. per week.

     „    „  2 children 4s. 10d. „   „

     „    „ 4   „    5s. 0d. „   „

Nurses for the children are provided without any extra charge. At present the Home does little more than cover working expenses, and for that reason no inducement is offered to other municipalities to copy the example of Glasgow.

3.—**The Block Dwelling.** This covers a variety of buildings, but the essential feature

is a many-storied house, with common approach
and (often) common conveniences, intended to
accommodate a varying number of separate
families. This sort of dwelling was thought by
early housing reformers to be the panacea for
all our housing ills, for it seemed to offer a
way out of the two great difficulties which
face those who seek to build houses in all large
cities, *viz.* (a) the extreme scarcity of land for
building sites and (b) the lack of quick and cheap
transport from the suburbs to the centre, where
the dwellers have to work. As one of these earlier
reformers put it, " Surely the heavens are high,
and if buildings can no longer stretch in a hori-
zontal direction, let them rise aloft toward the
silent stars ! "

Accordingly this type of building was largely
resorted to, not only on the Continent, where it is
a special feature of such cities as Berlin, Paris,
but in Scotland (typically in Glasgow) and the
United States. More than a quarter of a million of
people live in such dwellings in London; and there
are large numbers thus accommodated in Liverpool, Manchester and Nottingham, in which cities
the local authorities have thus housed workers in
accordance with Part III. of the Housing Act.

4.—Objections to " Block Dwellings."
There is now, amongst housing reformers everywhere, and especially in England, a growing feeling
against this type of building and for the following
reasons. (a) In the first place, such "barrack"
dwellings do not really give the comfort and

decency of a separate home. With the same approach and, oftentimes, the sharing of sanitary conveniences, with the lack of garden or separate back yard, little home privacy can be obtained ; and this is a very serious loss, especially to the child life. A recent writer has well summed up this objection in the words : " In a block dwelling an element of the impersonal and the inhuman seems to brood over every quarter. We have indeed the machine-made house ! " (b) But there is a stronger objection still to this type of dwelling in the fact, which the vital statistics reveal, that they are seriously detrimental to the health of the tenants.* This has now been established beyond question, so that it is unnecessary to give any additional proof. We need only refer readers to such a well-known authority on this subject as Dr. J. F. J. Sykes, if they wish to pursue it in detail.†

The reasons for this bad bill of health are not far to seek—the lack of sunshine and fresh air, especially in the lower storeys of block dwellings ; the many stairs which have to be climbed up and

* Cf. *e.g.* Report of Proceedings at the Annual Meeting of the Glasgow Workmen's Dwellings Co. (October 31st, 1906). Where in a total number of inhabitants in houses, most of which are blocks, " The average (death-rate for 1906) for the whole of the houses was 27.6, while the average for Glasgow in 1905 was 17.9."

† Cf. *Public Health and Housing, e.g.* p. 36 : " The phthisis death-rate shows a close relationship to density of persons in cubic space, and phthisis appears to stand almost in the same relationship to respiratory-pollution as typhoid fever does to filth pollution." And Cf. pp. 56-66.

H

down before work or recreation can be reached (a much more serious objection than would at first sight appear), the too close contact in case of infection, and the impossibility of sufficiently isolating cases of un-notifiable but seriously infectious diseases such as consumption and cancer.

5.—Cost of Block Dwellings. The last objection to be raised against these block dwellings is that they are very costly to erect and also to manage. Although sites are so expensive in the centre of our large cities yet, builders tell us, the extreme cost of block dwellings is due more to the expense of construction than to that of the site. In fact it is stated that a dwelling of the same number of rooms on the " block " system will cost just double the amount for construction as that on the two-storey cottage system. Thus, except in the case where the site is extremely expensive, the former type of building is condemned on the point of cost alone. Management in such large buildings, too, is a difficult matter and consequently high salaries have to be paid to men efficient for such work. All these objections have led housing reformers to reject the idea of this type of building as a satisfactory cure of our housing evils; in fact, in the case of Liverpool, the Town Council has openly decided against this system for the future.

6.—The Tenement House. Yet a fourth type of workers' dwellings is that which is known as the *Tenement House*. This is an improvement on the Block Dwellings for the Tenement House (in England though not in the United States) is never more than three, and often only two storeys high. Three or four, or at most six, families occupy such a house, so that there is by no means that same amount of publicity which makes Block Dwellings so objectionable. But the approach and such conveniences as back-yard, scullery, etc., are usually for common use, which is again a serious objection to this type of dwelling. The construction of such houses, however, is much less costly than that of "blocks," and often old houses in neighbourhoods that have deteriorated are adapted for the purpose. Management, also, is a less considerable item. Consequently rents are usually lower for rooms in tenements than in "blocks," whilst more privacy can be secured in the former than in the latter type of dwelling.

7.—The Cottage Flat. The *Cottage Flat* is the fifth type of working-class dwelling. This is always a two-storied building, containing an upper and lower completely self-contained flat. Each of these flats is built for only one family and there is a separate entrance on to the street for each of the families, and often separate gardens or yards. It will at once be seen that such an arrangement meets the objections we have raised against block and tenement buildings. All the privacy of a true home, as also the maximum of sunshine and fresh air which the site can receive, are secured to the inhabitants. The cost, too, of construction is much less than that of block dwellings, as we have already seen. If, then, a separate cottage cannot

be supplied to each worker and his family, this
arrangement is surely the one to be sought after
by housing reformers.   Thus in Birmingham, as
far back as 1892, cottage flats were built in Ryder
Street and Milk Street by the Corporation, and
have since been let at a rent of from 5/6 to 6/6
per flat.   Similar cottage flats have been more
recently erected at Hornsey where the scheme has
been quite a financial success and there are always
scores of applications for the first vacancy.   But
it is to Richmond that we must look for the most
successful experiment, by a Corporation, in this
direction.   Here have been built, as a result of
the energy and initiation of Alderman Thompson,
more than a hundred and thirty such cottage flats.
These flats accommodate over 600 persons under
perfectly healthy conditions and at a rent considerably lower than was being paid for much
inferior accommodation.   There has been a net
profit throughout the experiment, and this is
being put to a sinking fund which will eventually
secure to the Richmond municipality the whole of
the property.

   8.—The Separate Dwelling-house.   The
sixth and last type of dwelling is the ordinary,
separate cottage or dwelling-house.   This, of
course, is the most desirable dwelling for a worker
and his family.   It is needless here to point out its
many advantages over the other dwellings we have
mentioned.   One of the chief of these is the fact
that each cottage can have that touch of individuality which Mr. Charles Booth rightly reckons so

important in the construction of a home.* The
chief difficulty is that the cost is almost prohibitive to the labourer who earns less than £1
per week.

We have now to review the sources from which
this various supply of dwellings comes.

9.—**Employers' Housing.** Some have been
built by employers for their men, but the supply from
this source has been for many years now steadily
decreasing. The "tied cottage" has been found
to create an altogether dependent position for the
worker-tenant and has consequently been less
and less useful. The exception to this rule is
where the employer removes his factory from the
town to the country and, consequently, has to
migrate his workpeople and supply them with
cottages. In our rural districts this failure of
employers' housing has been intensified owing to
the increased difficulty experienced by the landowner in erecting cottages at a price which will
bring in any return at the highest rent that can
be charged.

As we have already seen, private enterprise, too,
has very largely failed to supply the required
number of dwellings at a possible rent. This has
been due to many causes, amongst which we must
reckon the increased cost of labour, of building
materials (amounting to as much as 30 per cent.

---

*Cf. Final Vol. : " I wish I could rouse in the minds of
speculative builders a sense of the money value that lies in
individuality, with its power of attracting the eye, rooting the
affections, and arousing pride in house and home," p. 78.

during the last twenty years) and of land generally, also more stringent bye-laws and more
careful inspection.

10.—Semi-Private Building Companies. A
good many semi-private Building Companies have
accordingly gone in for supplying this want of
accommodation.   Such companies as The Peabody Trust, The East End Dwellings Co., The
Artizans' Dwelling Co. and The Co-partnership
Tenants' Housing Council—all of which limit
the rate of interest to their shareholders—have
erected a large number of working-men's dwellings
in or near London, and in other parts of the
country.   During the last ten years or more,
however, there has been a considerable falling off
in the activity of certain of these companies,
affected by the increased cost of labour, building
materials and land.   The various working-class
building societies have also undoubtedly helped to
supply the demand for accommodation.

11.—Municipal Housing. Hence many have
looked to the municipality to fill the gap still
left.   There are two main arguments directed
against this form of supply.   The first is that if
the municipality builds it deals a serious blow
against the builders as a class.   Private enterprise cannot be expected to successfully compete
with the municipality in this matter.   If the
municipality insists thus on building, it is urged, it
will only be increasing the evil of lack of accommodation, for private enterprise will tend to be
driven out of the field.   The answer to this

objection is that the need for accommodation is so urgent and extensive that there is plenty of room for both private and municipal enterprise. As a matter of fact private enterprise has not been shown to be especially failing during the last ten years and it must be remembered that it is only during that time that there has been any considerable development of municipal housing in this country. It was owing to the failure of private enterprise to supply the need *before that time* that made the London County Council resolve in 1895 to build for itself rather than let to Artizan Dwelling Companies for this purpose.

But the other main objection urged against municipal housing is that the municipality is not in a proper position to do this work. The municipality is a public body conferring a "sectional benefit" if it build houses for one class of its citizens. If the building scheme should not pay there is a great temptation to fall back upon the rates and thus further injure the whole body of citizens. A way will thus be open to all sorts of jobbery and corruption, already a serious danger to public bodies. Besides, it is urged, a public body like the municipality is not in the position to give that infinite variety of accommodation which the housing of the people demands. Only the ordinary business pressure of competition and the rising of supply to the level of demand, with a view to commercial profit, will give this variety; and the municipality is not able to compete or to meet this demand as the private builder would. In answer to this it may be retorted that so far from municipal housing, when properly managed, being a "sectional benefit" it is a real and distinct benefit to the whole community. Recalling the illustration we have already given of the Richmond scheme, an illustration which can be repeated from London, Glasgow, Liverpool, Birmingham and many other cities, we saw there that the whole body of ratepayers gained the reversion, in a few years, of a valuable building estate for which they had not paid a penny. There is also the fact that the residents on this estate are all paying the town rates, thus helping to bear the general burden of the community. As to the temptation to have recourse to the rates for housing experiments, this is only the case in such schemes as are part of a large public improvement like the Boundary Street Clearance. For instance, one of the standing orders of the London County Council on ordinary housing schemes includes the words, "There shall be no charge on the county rate in respect of the dwellings in such area or scheme."

12.—The Public Health and Slum Areas. Slum removal, on the other hand, and the provision of wholesome accommodation are surely as much matters of public health as sanitary inspection and hospital isolation, the expense of which is met by the rates ! Dr. Smart, Professor of Political Economy in the University of Glasgow, who is by no means partial to Municipal Housing, admits the truth of this view. "There is no centre," he says, "of material deterioration

and infection worse than an insanitary house.
. . . Looking at these things, it would be
easy to argue that, even if we lose—even if the
loss come on the rates—it is the purchase-money
for a national gain."*

While there is this real danger to the public
health from such insanitary areas in our cities
(and also in many of our rural districts, as we have
seen), and while there still exists a real house
famine in our land there is surely a clear call to
local authorities to exercise, judicially and wisely,
the rights of building given them under the Housing
of the Working Classes Act.

13.— **Municipal Housing of the Poor.**
There only remains, then, the question:—For
what class exactly is the municipality to provide
accommodation? This is a question which, of
course, will vary in different places. In some
towns and many villages the local authority will
doubtless have to build for the working class as a
whole; this will be where the house famine is at

* Cf. pp. 8, 9 and 10 of *The Housing Problem and the
Municipality*, by William Smart, LL.D. (Adshead, Glasgow. 1d.) "We have a very large poor population.
Out of 156,000 occupied houses, 36,000 are one-roomed
houses and 70,000 are two-roomed houses. Of these, over
21,000 are ticketed houses accommodating 78,000 persons.
The ticketed houses are, I believe, an institution peculiar to
Glasgow. Any house not exceeding three rooms, if its total
cubic capacity does not exceed 2,000 ft., may, on measure-
ment by the sanitary inspector, have a small metal ticket
affixed to the door, giving the total cubic contents and the
legal maximum of inmates allowed. . . . Twelve per
cent. of these ticketed houses are habitually overcrowded.
About 2,000 of them are in an insanitary state. These are
our slums."

its worst, and where private enterprise cannot or will not increase the supply of houses. In other places, and probably in most of our largest cities, the municipality may have to restrict its attention to some special class of our workers. Professor Smart argues that it is clearly impossible, *e.g.* in Glasgow, where " there is an annual influx of some 10,000 souls into the city, all requiring house room," for the municipality to attempt to build for the whole working class population, and he urges the importance of distinguishing two classes amongst these, *viz.* the "decent" and the " dissolute" poor. For the first of these classes it is undesirable for the municipality to build ; it is the presence of the latter class that makes rent go up for all alike, and turns many good streets into slums. His suggestion, therefore, is that the corporation should " build for the dissolute poor, and make it impossible for them to get a footing anywhere else. In asking the Corporation to build, we are bound to recognize that all it can do in the way of housing is quite insignificant, and, this being so, care must be taken that nothing is done to check private enterprise in the immensely larger work of providing houses for the poorer classes generally. . . . It is, then, for the improvident and destructive, but not criminal, class that I ask the Corporation to build." In Liverpool the Town Council has made an interesting experiment in this direction. The very cheapest form of building consistent with durability has been constructed for this class. An average rent of little

more than a 1s. per room is charged; there are no
sort of decorations, and only the barest conveniences in the tenements, which are found to let
well and just cover expenditure. While agreeing
with Professor Smart as to the necessity of housing
the "poorest poor," we must be guided by circumstances in each case, and many of the further
experiments that have been made by municipalities
cannot but command our approval.

14.—**Does Municipal Housing Pay ?** "Does
municipal housing pay?" is a question that is
frequently asked. That it *has* paid in some cases
we have already seen. But there is no doubt that
the fact that so very few local authorities use their
housing powers under the Act of 1890 is due to the
difficulty of this question of finance. The burden
of the rates is so heavy to-day that any suggestion
which may further increase that burden is extremely
unpopular. So nothing is said, in many districts,
about the need, although so apparent, for housing
schemes. The stringent conditions of the Local
Government Board, the increased cost of labour
and of materials all help to encourage this inaction
on the part of our municipal bodies.

15.—**Repayment of Loans.** It is largely,
however, because municipalities have found
it such a serious task to be responsible for
the repayment of Government loans in thirty
or forty years, that much hesitation is shown in
building houses for workmen. A good return
can easily be made on money spent to cover
interest on loans, repairs, management expenses

and rates and taxes. But in addition to all this, sufficient return has to be made to add annually to a Sinking Fund intended to repay the initial loan. This is the difficulty which keeps many local authorities back from any housing enterprise, and it is a difficulty which might be overcome. If the land purchased by the municipality were regarded as an asset, which undoubtedly it is, the amount it cost could and should be met by the ratepayers as a whole. It is they who will be entire owners of this land when the loan has been repaid, and it is they, therefore, who should bear the burden of extinguishing the debt. This arrangement would leave the municipality free to seek repayment only on the interest, repairs, management, and rates and taxes. To further lighten the repayment of the loans, which will now fall upon the ratepayers' shoulders, Government should extend the statutory time from 60 years to 100 years for land and, perhaps, 80 years for buildings. A more reasonable reform than this of the extension of the years for repaying Government loans could not be cited. In the Hornsey housing scheme it has been estimated that all the rents of the cottages could be reduced by 9d. per week if this simple reform were put into operation. A saving of 3d. per week in each £100 outlay would also be effected under similar conditions at Richmond.

16.—**Rate of Interest.** Another much needed reform in this direction is the reduction of the rate of interest at which most municipalities are able

to borrow of the Government. The 3, or more
often, 3½ and 4 per cent. which such bodies must
pay for housing loans ought to be reduced to 2½
per cent., the rate at which the Government pays
the working classes for their investments in the
Savings Bank Funds—with perhaps another ½ per
cent. added to cover the necessary charges.
Many reformers are looking towards these Funds
and asking why they should not be used on a
large scale for housing schemes as in Belgium.

We have appended* a Memorandum on Practical Points of Housing Reform, drawn up by the
National Housing Reform Council, and presented
to the Parliamentary Committee of the same
Council for their consideration and adoption.
Much of the programme of reform here laid down
will meet with the warm approval of housing reformers of all shades of political faith.

* See Appendix, No. I.

# CHAPTER VIII.

## GARDEN CITIES AND SUBURBS.

---

"We all need space; unless we have it we cannot reach that sense of quiet in which whispers of better things come to us gently." (Miss Octavia Hill.)

"Houses blessed with gardens—a wonderful influence." (*From an Investigator's Reports in Charles Booth's book.*)

---

WE have pointed out, in a previous chapter on "Rural Housing and Depopulation," that the exodus from the country districts to the towns seems to be due to economic and not merely to accidental causes. We have also shown that between the years 1881–1901 no less than 244 new urban districts were created in England, a fact which illustrates the strong tendency to-day towards town and city-making. The originators of the Garden City scheme fully recognize this tendency. "Let us go on making cities, by all means," they say, "but let us make *beautiful* cities! Let us make cities which shall combine the advantages of industrial and rural life!" This

118

is the spirit of the Garden City movement, a movement which not only our desire for social betterment, but actual facts seem to warrant us in saying has come to stay.

It is a movement which seeks to make us ashamed of our ugly, unhealthy cities, and to advance principles by which the worst evils may be altogether abolished, or at least reduced to a minimum, in the planning of new cities. As a recent writer on the subject * points out, our rural districts are perhaps the most beautiful in Europe, the gentle undulating character of English landscape lending them a peculiar charm; but, on the other hand, our cities and many of our larger towns are hopelessly unlovely, and hardly bear comparison with the towns of Germany, where every third or even fourth-rate city has well laid-out gardens, open spaces, broad streets and fine municipal buildings.

1.—Advantages of Garden Cities. The main principles of this new movement, then, may be classified as follows :—(1) Since most of our cities are growing in a haphazard way and becoming increasingly ugly, the only effective cure for this is to start afresh—to build cities that shall not be allowed to expand except along stated lines, and these lines in the direction of the maximum of beauty obtainable. As the official handbook of The First Garden City Co. puts it: "The essence of the idea lies in the principle of beginning at the

* The *Edinburgh Review*, October, 1905.

beginning. Instead of allowing houses to be run
up here and there, one block or one street quite
irrespective of the position of another, drainage
and water systems being introduced piecemeal, as
best they can . . . the whole city which is to be,
should be planned out from the outset with an eye
to the convenience of the community as a whole." *
Those who advocate this principle point out how
many of the blunders and disfigurements of our
towns could have been avoided by a little fore-
thought and previous arrangement. They give
instances of such lack of planning or restriction—
*e.g.* the hopeless suburban, working-class areas
which are being created in West Ham, Walthamstow and Willesden around London—and ask if
it would not have been possible a few years back
to have made such areas more habitable or even
beautiful. They show that it would have been
quite easy but for that lack of initiative and
imagination which is so marked a characteristic
of the English people. Accordingly they desire
to establish one example of how a city should be
planned and its development controlled. Hence
the advisability of a new start, an entirely fresh
experiment, allowing all legitimate conclusions to
be drawn from it.

(2.) But the second principle of the Garden
City is perhaps more important still, because it
touches so closely that particular phase of
our social life to which we have already referred.

* " The Garden City Movement," G. Montagu Harris,
M.A., p. 21.

For good or ill we are a manufacturing people, and any new scheme for the better housing of the community must recognize at the outset this essential condition. The advocates of the Garden City profess that their scheme entirely allows for this economic fact. The chief end of the Garden City is to be a town where all the ordinary industries of commercial life may be carried on, but where the usual modern disadvantages of such industries are to be absent. "It must be clearly understood that *the main object* of the Garden City movement is to make it possible for industries to be carried on under conditions favourable to the health of the people employed in them."* It is contended that these conditions, advantageous as they will be to employees, will be also advantageous to manufacturers. "The healthier the workman, the more and the better work can he do, while a decent home in pleasant surroundings is, to the sort of man a manufacturer wants, an additional attraction to regular work and good wages." Thus, to answer the demand of the employer, there will be a good supply of well-housed, healthy and contented workers. If all our large industrial centres had such a labouring class to draw from, what would the commercial gain be, not only to the employers, but to the community at large?

(3.) The third principle underlying the Garden City enterprise is also of the utmost importance to the country generally. The promoters of this

* "The Garden City Movement," p. 27.

I

movement seek to use to the full the great advantages which arise from the municipalisation of the land. All the immense value, which belongs to urban land when it becomes the scene of industrial activity, will, in garden cities, accrue to the community which creates this value. It is upon the "unearned increment" that the financial foundation of the Garden City scheme really rests. This important portion of the wealth of our country has, for some time past, been closely observed by social reformers. In the Garden City of the future what has been gained by the activities of the community is to be for the use of the community. All improvement in the value of the sites in the Garden City will go towards lowering the rates or furthering the residential advantages of the "city" in general. In some other countries of Europe, notably Germany, the advantage of the city holding its own land for its own profit has long been recognized. We here in England have been very slow in learning from these examples. It seems as though a new, and perhaps at last an unanswerable, argument for municipalising the land on a large scale were to be presented in the first Garden City.

2.—The First Garden City Company. But let us consider the first example, which has already come into existence, of this new movement. In 1899 the Garden City Association was formed to bring before the public the principles which we have stated. This, by 1902, had been so successful in its propaganda, and had attracted to itself such considerable public support, that the Garden City Pioneer Co. Ltd. was formed with about £20,000 for capital. This company a year later took the first practical steps towards realising the desired end. Under the title of The First Garden City Co. Ltd. it purchased a site, and started all the necessary machinery for developing what is now a large and growing enterprise. The estate, destined to be the site of the First Garden City, was excellently chosen. It lies, as nearly everybody now knows, some thirty miles from London and twenty miles from Cambridge, not far distant from the town of Hitchin in Hertfordshire. A visit to this delightful spot well repays the time and trouble, and every facility is offered by the Great Northern Railway Company, which has already opened a temporary station at Letchworth called " Garden City." Nearly 4,000 acres of land have been purchased on high ground, and it has all been carefully surveyed and planned out according to the principles which the Garden City Association has advocated. This large estate was bought at the low rate of £40 per acre so that the full benefit of cheap purchase of land should accrue to the community which, it is hoped, will soon form the First Garden City. The full advantage of the 'unearned increment" is also reserved to the community by the stipulation that shareholders shall receive at no time more than 5% interest on their investment. All the chief roads and avenues are already mapped out, and no part of the estate is let to any company or individual without the most stringent restrictions as to building plans. True to the idea of joining industrial with country life it has been arranged that only 1,200 of the 3,808 acres shall be used for the site of the actual city. Round this smaller site will be grouped the agricultural land of the community and also the land upon which the various factories will be situated. This is a most important part of the scheme and for its success, it is obvious, there will have to be the help of a considerable number of our larger employers of labour. Already nearly a dozen firms have erected factories on this part of the estate and most of the workpeople employed will find a permanent home in the Garden City. The total population of the " City " is about 3,000, among which number must be reckoned the few hundred original inhabitants of two hamlets which the estate includes. The limit of population has been] fixed at 35,000, leaving the density on the estate area at about nine per acre, on the town area at twenty-three per acre.

3.—The Cheap Cottages Exhibition. We need not here describe in detail the housing projects which are already being carried out. A very successful Cheap Cottages Exhibition was held on the estate in October, 1905, and in these cottages, and in fact in every new building on the estate, the utmost care has been taken to secure for the inhabitants the best housing conditions at the lowest cost.

Of course, it is early yet to speak of the success

of this interesting experiment; its greatest needs at present are :—(1) Generous financial aid ; (2) The support of manufacturing firms, following the present tendency of removing large factories from our cities to rural districts ; (3) An increased population. If ever this experiment becomes a real and permanent success, as all interested in the better housing of the people sincerely hope, a very significant step in the right direction will have been taken.

4.—**Bournville.** Although Letchworth Estate is, as we have seen, the first experiment on the precise lines of a " Garden City," there are, in actual existence, villages which have all the essential features of such a " city." The most important of these is the model village of Bournville, near Birmingham. Here, through the munificence and foresight of Mr. George Cadbury who has made a free gift of the whole site to the community, is in full working order a little township identical in aim and ideals with that towards which the Letchworth pioneers are labouring. A Public Trust has the entire charge and management of the village, all the housing conditions are dictated by this Trust and are of the most perfect kind.

The main conditions of the Trust Deed with regard to the letting of land are as follows :—

(A) *Houses* to be either semi-detached or in blocks of four. Dwellings to occupy only about one-quarter of sites. 600 square yards of garden.

(B) *Factories* not to occupy more than one-fifteenth of whole estate.

(C) *Land.*—

   (1) To be let on 999 years' lease.
   (2) Cottages on it not to be sold outright. (They are now let at weekly rents by the Trust.)
   (3) A small ground rent.
   (4) Covenants in the leases.
   (5) Money on mortgage at 2½ to 3%.

5.—**A great Housing Experiment.** The rents are, at the same time, by no means " philanthropic," for the very essence of the idea is that Bournville should be an experiment such as any municipalities wishing to house the working classes at a paying rent might imitate. As a matter of fact the founder himself expressly stated this principle on the completion of his generous gift. "The public announcement," he said, "of the experiment would not have been made just now (1901) had it not been for the fact that the London County Council and other important municipal bodies are preparing great housing schemes, and that I feel so strongly that it would be a lamentable mistake to herd working people together in localities other than those they now occupy, thereby creating more slums." Bournville has certainly demonstrated that the housing of the working classes in thoroughly good, sanitary and even beautiful cottages (with gardens attached), is quite possible, and that a fair return of 4 per cent. can be made on the capital to cover ground rent, rates and taxes, repairs and total management. How wonderfully well this experiment has worked out only a visit to the charming village itself can fully show. But in proof of its success we may mention the following facts :—(1) the cottages are never vacant but there is a keen competition for renting them at 5/- and upward per week; (2) the general pride taken in the appearance of the interior of the houses and especially of the gardens is everywhere apparent; (3) there is practically no loss owing to arrears of rent ; (4) more than half of the inhabitants of the village are not engaged, as might be expected, in the famous cocoa works at Bournville but work in Birmingham and the surrounding districts and have come to Bournville, attracted by the housing conditions; and, (5) last but not least, the health of this community of men and women is extraordinarily good, the death rate being less than 10 per 1,000 (8 per 1,000 in 1903) as against the average of 20 per 1,000 in the neighbouring Birmingham. "The infant mortality figures for Bournville (65 per 1,000) are such that, if they applied to the whole kingdom, the lives of at least 50,000 infants would be saved annually " | *

A similar experiment, modelled to some extent on that of Mr. Cadbury, has been made by Mr. Joseph Rowntree, the Chairman of Rowntree & Co., Ltd. The Village Trust, to which he has

* See Report of Co-operative Congress Visit to Bournville Village. Leaflet to be had of the Secretary, 18, Dulverton Road, Leicester.

transferred 120 acres of land at Earswick, West
Huntingdon, two miles from York, has already
constructed between 40 and 50 houses which
would serve as a model to any municipality
building working class cottages.   In the deed of
foundation, as at Bournville, one-tenth of the land,
exclusive of roads, is to be laid out and used as
parks, recreation grounds and open spaces.   The
houses are not to occupy more than one-fourth of
the sites upon which they are built, and most of
the houses already constructed have gardens of
not less than 350 square yards.   There are strips
of grass of about 5 ft. wide between the roadway
and the footpath on each side, and on these strips
trees have been planted.   The houses are let at
about 4s. 6d. per week, the tenants paying the
rates, which amount to 8d. per week.   It is hoped
that the experiment will be a useful contribution
to the housing problem, and since the nett rental
of the houses amounts to about 3½ per cent. on
the capital expended, there seems good reason for
supposing that any local authority, without inflicting a burden upon the rates, might advantageously
follow the example set at Earswick.

Very much the same sort of conditions obtain
in Port Sunlight, the model village where Messrs.
Lever Brothers have established their famous
soap works and housed their workers; and, only
to mention one foreign example, the model
colonies of Messrs. Krupp & Co.   These all are
examples where workers in large industrial
enterprises are being well and profitably

housed. Those responsible for these schemes assure us that not only is a reasonable return made upon the large outlay of capital necessary, but that they are otherwise thoroughly paying concerns in the increased vigour, happiness and general efficiency of the workers whom they seek to benefit.

The "Garden City" principle, if we may so call it, is being worked out in several other directions. There are a few private companies devoted to the development of small estates along these lines, some of them introducing the element of Co-partnership.

6.—The Ealing Tenants Ltd. The Ealing Tenants Ltd.* is the most flourishing of these Co - partnership Housing Companies. This Company holds property to the value of over £50,000, most of which is [situated on a well-developed estate at Ealing. Two years ago a similar Company was formed in connection with the Garden City at Letchworth under the title of the Garden City Tenants. This company has leased various parts of the Letchworth estate from Garden City Ltd., and is proceeding to develop these properties which are valued at more than £30,000. Similar Companies have been or are being formed at Sevenoaks, Birmingham, Berkhampstead, Oxford, and Guildford.

7.—Co-partnership in Housing. Such co-partnership in the holding of small estates results in

* Like the "Garden City Tenants Ltd." it was originated by the Co-partnership Tenants Housing Council.

the advantages of cheaper land, cheaper conveyance
of this land, and cheaper building upon it—all
secured on the familiar principle of "reduction on
quantity." But the greatest advantage that such
ownership has over private ownership is that some
amount of development and planning is possible.
This, as we have seen, is one of the salient
features of the " Garden City." " As soon as
the element of Co-partnership is introduced and
some acres of ground get developed with a view to
realising some consistent scheme and producing
some definite effect, very much wider opportunity
(than in individual effort) is afforded. Advantage
may be taken of spots of interest or beauty on the
ground. Houses may be grouped around these
spots, around open greens, or in many other such
ways as may be arranged to take advantage of
aspect and outlook by departing a little from the
usual regular plot, and in addition to sharing the
responsibilities and profits of house owning, it
becomes easy to arrange for the tenants to share
also the enjoyment of open spaces, tennis lawns,
play-grounds for children, and particularly beautiful spots or views which could not be secured
to a series of detached individuals." *

So far as Co-operative Societies generally are
concerned, it should be remembered that, notwithstanding the enormous difficulties confronting
them in the towns, they have already done much

* " Co-partnership in Housing from an Architect's Standpoint " ; paper in " Garden Suburbs, Villages and Homes " :
Raymond Unwin. (Garden City Press, 6d.)

to provide decent cottages for their members. It
is not possible to obtain exact figures, but it is
estimated that over 25,000 houses have been built
at a cost of nearly £5,000,000.

8.—**The Garden Suburb.** One other movement we must mention, a movement which is only
just being organised, but which seeks to deal with
existing towns and cities and to prevent their
suburbs becoming ugly under the hand of the
speculating builder. The Garden Suburb movement is much like what we have attempted already
to describe, but that it seeks to improve existing
towns rather than to make a fresh start elsewhere.
Mrs. Barnett's plan for a Garden Suburb on and
near land recently added to Hampstead Heath
has received much support, and already an estate
of 240 acres has been purchased, upon which a
model suburb is to be built.* This is to be run,
like Bournville, on sound financial lines, and it is
hoped that it will also, like Bournville, prove a
great success.

9.—**The value of the Garden.** Such are the
efforts being made towards creating Garden
suburbs or villages where the Garden City itself is
beyond reach. The common element in all such
efforts is proper planning and plenty of garden
space, an essential if we are to preserve our
industrial centres from becoming nightmares of
civilisation. "Half the evil of the strain of

* See article by Mrs. Barnett in *Progress*—the organ of
the British Institute of Social Service, 11, Southampton
Row, W.C.

commercial occupation is due to excitement, to tension of the mind. The garden in which actual personal work can be done in the evening and on holidays, is the most restful of all places. The mother needs the solace of sweet and quiet surroundings and the opportunity of getting often into the fresh air without having to prepare for formal outings. As for the children, the garden is the one supreme opportunity of giving them a happy, healthy life from the first." * Such gardens it must be our aim to secure for the people in village, town and city.

* " The Need for Home Gardens," Edward Owen Greening in " Garden Suburbs, Villages and Homes."

# CHAPTER IX.

## THE PROBLEM OF TRANSIT.

" The evils resulting from slow and imperfect means of locomotion appear to us to be quite as serious from a social as from an economic point of view." (*Royal Commission on London Traffic*, 1905.)

THE distribution of population in a commercial city is wholly different from the distribution of population in an industrial city. Special facili-. ties for rapid transit are required in each case. We are dealing more especially with industrial conditions in this chapter, and it is now recognised that with the immense growth of our big industrial towns all the restrictions which have been placed in the way of the pressure outwards from the centre to the circumference, must be removed or the life of the city will become clogged and hopelessly complicated.

Nearly all our old towns were built without plan or design, nor had the original builders contemplated the rapid growth of population as the

result of the industrial revolution. Who would
have believed that the narrow streets in the centre
of the city of London would one day have to
serve a population of 5,000,000 inhabitants? A
hundred years ago many of the street widenings
now so necessary could have been effected for a
comparatively small sum of money. To-day the
price is prohibitive, and not even the City
Corporation or the London County Council could,
if they would, enter upon the immense outlay
which wholesale widenings would involve.

The process of growth of a great city is essen-
tially a movement on economic lines, but this,
unfortunately, does not imply any definite plan of
growth nor does it imply that the means of transit
will grow with equal rapidity. If an industrial
city with a huge aggregation of population is to
be healthy, the centrifugal force should be equal
to the centripetal—that is to say, facilities must be
offered for the working out of the economic law
by which business is transacted in the centre of
the city where land is dear and the worker lives
on the outskirts where it is cheap.

Is there any natural or economic limit to a
city's size? Aristotle's ideal city was 10,000 in
number; but there were ten times as many in
London in the reign of Queen Elizabeth. It seems
impossible to predict to what size, under modern
conditions, a city may not grow. Inner London,
with its population of 1½ millions, 25 per cent.
living in overcrowded conditions, is only typical
of all the capitals of the world—Paris, Berlin,

New York, etc. The latter city, for example, despite facilities for locomotion, on one piece of land between 14th Street and East of the Bowery only 979 acres in extent, has a population of 455,000 or 465 to the acre, and although this state of things is rather exceptional, yet in a lesser degree a similar problem will be found in nearly all big industrial centres.

1.—Royal Commission on London Traffic, 1905. A subject that has the closest and most direct bearing upon the housing question is that of locomotion and transport. The Royal Commission appointed to inquire into the means of locomotion and transport in London gave to the public last year eight large volumes, some of them containing over a thousand pages. Judged by the size and weight of this " handy little manual " it would be impossible to exaggerate the importance of facilitating locomotion in London. We have already pointed out that the working classes cannot be housed in the central area at rents which they can afford to pay, and so the whole problem of London locomotion, and for the matter of that, the transit question of most large towns, needs to be dealt with on a comprehensive plan, and as speedily as possible.

Let us take a few of the points of the Royal Commission as they affect the housing of the working classes—points which were clearly established by a mass of indisputable evidence.

(a) That overcrowding in the metropolitan district is, generally speaking, greatest in the central area, and tends to diminish towards the suburbs.

(*b*) In this central area the average weekly rents for workmen's dwellings are very high and tend to diminish towards the suburbs.

(*c*) The price of land in the central districts of London is too high to allow it to be used for re-housing purposes.

(*d*) That many workmen can, if transport be provided, live outside the central area.

(*e*) That where facilities for locomotion have been provided the population does as a matter of fact take advantage of them, and live either in the suburbs or outside London proper.

1.—**Five Important Points.** Let us consider these propositions one by one, and first as to the extent of overcrowding. (*a*) The Statistical Officer of the London County Council points out in the tables furnished by him, that the population per acre in the central area of London is 148, and in the rest of the county (excluding North Woolwich), it is 54. In districts adjacent to the County (including North Woolwich), it is 16.6, and in the rest of greater London it is 2.5. About a million and a half of people live in the central, or most congested area, and the table * furnished by Mr. Harper shows clearly that speaking generally the overcrowding diminishes in accordance with the density of the population per acre.

(*b*) Taking the second point, that rents are higher

---

* Royal Commission Appendix No. 6, Table 2, p. 126, Vol. 3.

in the central district and tend to diminish towards the suburbs. Here again the figures of Mr. Harper show that in the central area the average weekly rent of working class houses, whether erected by the London County Council or by private enterprise, is 3s. 3½d. per room. In the rest of the county it is 2s. 4½d. and in the extra or greater London it is 2s. * This must be regarded strictly as the average, for there will probably be many exceptions on both sides, but the figures may be regarded as approximately correct.

(c) As to the third point that the land is too valuable for rehousing in central districts. There is no difficulty in showing that the working classes cannot afford to pay the rents which would have to be charged if the rehousing is to be made commercially profitable, and on the other hand we have a certain number of experiments which prove conclusively that land can be purchased a few miles out from the centre of London at a sufficiently low rate to admit of rehousing without loss, at rents which the tenants can afford to pay. To give two illustrations alone. In connection with the Holborn to the Strand improvement the Council was required to build workmen's dwellings in place of those that were demolished, and for this purpose they bought the Bourne Estate, the cost being £201,107. They were compelled to write this sum down to £44,000 and debit the balance to the cost of street improve-

* Royal Commission, Appendix No. 6, Table 9, p. 132, Vol. 3.

K

ments. If they had not done this it would have
been necessary to have charged rents which the
working classes could not possibly have paid.
Even as it is the rents are from 9s. 6d. to 11s. a
week for a three-room tenement. The buildings
erected will accommodate 2,640 persons, and
accordingly there is a loss of nearly £60 per head
of the persons rehoused, the whole of this loss
falling upon the rates. Contrast with this the
experiment made by the L.C.C. in purchasing
land at Tooting upon which to construct workmen's dwellings. The district can be approached
either by railway or the L.C.C. electric tramways,
and the three-roomed cottages built upon this land
are letting at rents from 7s. to 7s. 6d. per week,
and the scheme is entirely self-supporting. The
cost of land and of building on the Bourne Estate
per three-roomed tenement is £761 12s. 6d., as
compared with £263 10s. 0d. on the Tooting
Estate. What further illustration is required to
show the impossibility of rehousing in the central
area? Without any exception where the London
County Council has had to provide workmen's
dwellings in the central districts there has been a
heavy loss.* A table supplied by the London
County Council offers a comparison of the cost of
rehousing in the central area and building in
" Extra London." The result of the table shows
that in the central districts the ratepayers have
sustained a loss of £412,683 in rehousing 7,586

* Royal Commission, Appendix No. 6, pages 233 et seq.
Vol. 8.

persons on 18.55 acres, while in the suburbs the
Council has already housed 1,787 persons on 15
acres without any loss to the rates. That is to
say, on the one hand you have great waste of public
money and a congested population per acre, and on
the other, no loss of money at all, and a population
housed under fairly healthy conditions.

All the evidence goes to prove that it is far
better and cheaper to rehouse in the outer zones, if
cheap and rapid means of transit can be provided,
and it is for this reason that in 1903 the Local
Government Board was invested with powers
enabling them to authorise rehousing at a distance
from the demolished buildings, instead of in close
proximity as was formerly the case. It had
previously been discovered in former rehousing
schemes that it was not the same people who
were rehoused, and therefore the real object for
this expensive method of finding accommodation
was unnecessary. Of the 5,719 people displaced
in the Boundary Street area, only a small fraction
returned to the new dwellings.

(d) As to whether it is necessary for workers
to live near their work, Mr. Charles Booth
and Mr. W. Thompson both* think that it
should not be encouraged, and that in a very
large number of cases it is not necessary; but
of course it is obvious that there are some
trades and occupations, for example, that of
dockers, stevedores, market porters and night

* Questions 19087-90, Vol. 2. Royal Commission on
London Traffic. " The Housing Handbook," p. 221.

workers, in which any great distance between the
worker's place of residence and the work itself
would be an insuperable bar to employment.
There are also many cases where small factories
working long hours, especially in the cheap
tailoring trade, render near residence necessary,
but this is undesirable in itself, being a part of the
sweating system which needs to be attacked.
Generally speaking, we may say that providing
the accommodation is cheap and adequate, and
that the transit is speedy and likewise cheap, the
large majority of workers would be able to live
away from the immediate workshop or factory, in
the suburbs or on the outskirts of the town.

(*e*) And this is proved by the fact that where
facilities for locomotion have been afforded, the
population does in fact take advantage of them to
live in the outer suburbs.  The Royal Commission gives the two illustrations of Edmonton
and Walthamstow, both of which have largely
increased their. population since workmen's trains
were started.  The population of Edmonton
jumped from 14,000 when two workmen's trains
were started, to 62,000 when seven trains were
put on, and Walthamstow from 11,000 with two
trains, to 95,000 with eight trains.  We may
add that synchronising with the movement of
cheap trains, Inner London from 1891 to 1901
lost by emigration 494,000 persons, Middle
London gained 195,000 persons, and outer London
gained 1,200,000 persons.

As other special illustrations of the growth of

certain districts served by cheap trains, we may witness Leyton, Leytonstone, West Ham, East Ham, Tottenham and Enfield. The question of cheap transit by railway is, however, complicated by the fact that the Cheap Trains Act (1883) did not throw upon the Railway Companies the duty of opening up neighbourhoods for working class districts, but merely provided that such trains should be run when the demand for them existed. Where this demand exists there has been an extraordinary growth of population, a growth especially affecting the working classes and resulting in some injurious consequences. All the requirements of municipal life have to be rapidly supplied, houses let at a comparatively low rental prevent the construction of better class houses, and bring in only a small return. In Walthamstow 15,000 houses out of 18,600 are assessed at less than £16 a year. The rateable value is low and therefore the rates are high, and this is a problem which is engaging the attention of Parliament with reference to the Education rates in West Ham, East Ham and Tottenham.

3.—**Rapid Electric Transit.** Perhaps rapid electric transit is the most hopeful line upon which municipalities can move at the present time. Transit is a costly business, but nearly all municipal electric tramways pay, and if it were possible for the city to obtain some recoupment by the judicious acquisition of land beforehand along the main lines of proposed new tramways, a still larger profit would accrue, thus making these new routes a good investment. In all large industrial cities, electric trams are making an immense change. To give only one illustration out of many. The trams of Liverpool were electrified in 1899 and between 1900 and 1903, 6696 new houses were erected in added areas, an increase of 85 per cent., nearly all of them being artisans' dwellings from 6s. to 10s. per week, and taken up by city workmen. During this period the number of new houses built within the old city decreased by 40 per cent., and many of the so-called new houses were merely reconstructions of existing working-class dwellings by the Liverpool Corporation.

There is one other point which has not yet been touched on relative to the present unsatisfactory condition of things which exists when the factory is situated in the overcrowded part of the town. Those employed in the factory live as a rule in artisans' dwellings put up by a company or the municipality in close proximity to the workshop. The evil is two-fold. First it retains the factory in the centre when it should be removed to the outskirts of the city, and secondly it keeps the workers in the more overcrowded localities and keeps them there at the expense of the ratepayers who have rehoused at a loss. All housing reformers seem to be agreed that wherever possible the factory must be replaced by commercial business inside the town, and that in any case the people must not be allowed to establish themselves with overcrowded conditions in the centre.

London is a problem in itself of such magnitude

that the carrying out of any sufficient scheme of rapid transit would require the expenditure of many millions. Nevertheless, when we remember that greater London, in a comparatively short space of time, may have a population of over 10 millions, it will be seen that drastic remedies are required. As Mr. Charles Booth says : " Bolder engineering expedients can be adopted." Tube railways, sub-service tramways, mono-rail lines, workmen's trains, specialisation of streets for various forms of traffic, new avenues—all these questions are being considered in view of the change of population from ring to ring and zone to zone. Above all, existing highways must be broadened wherever possible, and all new main roads be constructed so as to allow of fast electric trams without in any way hindering ordinary vehicular traffic. To carry out all these schemes, for London at least, or to see that they are carried out in conformity with some definite plan, a Traffic Board must be appointed in accordance with the recommendation of the Royal Commission, or else the L.C.C. must be invested with far larger powers than are possessed by that public body at the present moment.

# CHAPTER X.

## GENERAL CONCLUSIONS.

———

" I will not cease from mental strife,
    Nor let the sword sleep in my hand,
  Till we have built Jerusalem
    In England's green and pleasant land."

(BLAKE.)

———

IN the foregoing chapters we have pointed out
the magnitude of the evils arising from bad
housing conditions; the rural depopulation and
urban overcrowding, the high death rates, and
especially great infant mortality, the disease and
sickness, which necessarily accompany overcrowding, the intemperance and the lunacy which are an
indirect effect of such conditions, the physical
deterioration and the ever-present problem of the
unemployable.

The remedies we have suggested, drastic as
some of them may seem to those who have never
studied the question, are not sufficiently drastic to
solve this problem for many years, even if put into
immediate operation, and we must be content to
go step by step, creating a sound public opinion
and carrying the people of this country with us in

all our reforms. We have no Baron Hausmann with power to reconstruct London as he, under the authority of Napoleon III., reconstructed Paris at the enormous cost of £48,000,000. Insanitary areas are being dealt with slowly. Very slowly also open spaces and parks are being added to London and our great cities. Large improvements have been effected in nearly all the principal towns of the country, but nevertheless, as it has been pointed out, the cost of big clearances in the centre of the town is absolutely prohibitive.

We summarise, however, the chief points, legislative and administrative, which the housing reformer would desire to emphasise. Most of them are along the line of least resistance and follow precedents which have already been set.

## No. 1.—Stricter Enforcement of the Health and Housing Acts.

Sound public opinion is required in order to overcome the inaction of local authorities. The outstanding loans of local authorities amount to £394,000,000, only four millions being set aside for building working men's dwellings. The President of the Local Government Board, Mr. John Burns, a short while ago issued a special circular urging an amendment of building bye-laws to facilitate the building of cheap but good cottages. Out of 667 Rural Councils, only about a dozen submitted new bye-laws in response to this circular, and these Councils are as inactive as ever.

The number of cases in which houses are reported as "unfit for human habitation" is comparatively small, when it is remembered the enormous number of dwellings (over five millions) under £15 in annual value. Only about ¼ of the Urban Councils have taken any action in this respect. This is not due to the fact that the town is immaculate as regards sanitation, but due rather to apathy and the *vis inertiæ* of vested interests.

In order to insure the carrying out of the existing Acts, the Local Government Board should institute a separate Health and Housing Department, with inspectors to visit the defaulting districts. These inspectors would advise the local authorities as to the means which might be adopted to remedy any existing abuses and would report all cases of neglect and inaction. In special cases where either the general Death Rate or the Infant Mortality was exceedingly high, the Local Government Board should institute a public enquiry. The same department should also make it possible for any small group of citizens in any district to call attention to nuisances and insanitary dwellings, and in this and some other respects the precedent of the Irish Labourers Act might well be followed. We append illustrations of the forms of representation under the Act of 1906.* It should also be possible for any district to take action under Part III. of the Housing of the Working Classes Act without the unnecessary preliminary of formal adoption.

* See Appendix No. II.

## No. 2.—Amendments Required in Existing Public Health and Housing Acts

(*a*) Compulsory house inspection should be a "sine qua non" wherever the death rate exceeds a certain percentage, and in order to discover the weak spots the town or district should be divided up into small sections by the Medical Officer of Health.

(*b*) The local authority should keep a register of all houses showing the size, number, and if possible, rent of the rooms, existing sanitary accommodation, and the general state of repair, together with the name of the owner of the site and the building. If this were done many a difficulty would be speedily remedied which otherwise might be postponed for months, or possibly years.

(*c*) The broadening of the definition of nuisances is required in order that houses may be included which have become dirty and dilapidated. The definition should also include rooms which do not afford a sufficient air space for each adult in each living-room and bedroom. The amount suggested is 500 cubic feet in the former case, and 400 in the latter.

(*d*) To insure the carrying out of their official work by the Medical Officers and Sanitary Inspectors, they should be required to give their whole time, and should not be removable except with the consent of the Local Government Board.

(*e*) Local authorities should be empowered to demolish houses unfit for human habitation within a certain date of the making of an order. Demolition at present is a long and tedious process.

(f) The clearance of slum areas should be made more possible by simplifying the procedure under Parts I. and II. of the Housing of the Working Classes Act, and compensation to the owners of slum property should be reduced to a minimum.

### No. 3.—Reforms in Rural Housing.

The chapter on rural housing quotes at some length the reforms suggested by the Select Committee on Housing, and it is only necessary briefly to state one or two of the most important. Apart from the points of reform already mentioned, *viz.* —the appointment of Medical Officers and Sanitary Inspectors only removable at the instance of the L.G.B., the transfer of powers to larger authorities, and the granting of facilities for making representation to the Local Government Board for special enquiries, there is needed power to enable local authorities to assist in the development of village life by encouraging the provision of cheap means of transit. It may be that this point is not of great importance as compared with transit in the town, but it has a distinct bearing upon life in the country, for if the village be inaccessible and isolated, not only is intercourse and trade rendered difficult, but the question of rates for the carriage of produce becomes an insuperable bar to the prosperity of that district. The prohibitive railway rate added to the cost of cartage to and from the railway makes it extremely difficult to place goods on the market at a reasonable price. If such means of transit could be provided it would be possible by establishing small holdings near the village, run upon co-operative lines, to greatly promote the prosperity of agriculture.

Since, however, one difficulty in our villages is the dearth of cottages (in many cases a primary cause of the rural exodus), not only must the rural local authorities be encouraged to build under Part III. of the Housing Act of 1890, but the Small Holdings Act should also be amended with a view to adding to the cottage such an amount of land as would make it possible for the tenant to pay what must be, under existing conditions, a fairly high rent for his cottage. At the same time money should be lent by the Government at a cheaper rate and for a longer period in order that the rent may be brought within the means of the agricultural labourer.

## No. 4.—Cheaper Money.

This question of cheaper money applies to the housing problem both in town and country. The restrictions which prevent the funds of savings banks and charities from being invested in housing schemes should be removed. This can be done without any loss whatever to the funds. The Public Works Loan Commissioners should at the same time loan money at the lowest market rate for housing purposes, up to say eighty years, to public bodies, and there seems no reason why they should not also lend money to recognised and well approved Co-operative Societies, building on municipal land and under municipal restrictions.

### No. 5.—Town Extension and Town Planning.

With a view to the proper development on right lines both of towns and of villages, local authorities or groups of local authorities, should be empowered not only to make plans for the future development of the land on the outskirts of the city or village, setting aside what is required for main roads, open spaces and sites for public buildings, but also to purchase land and large estates with a view to building cheap and suitable houses, or letting it under proper conditions for such purpose. The German model in this respect need not be exactly followed, but the principle should be adopted. If this land could be acquired by agreement, and at a fair price before the town was fully developed, the enhanced value of this land consequent on development, would make it possible for the local authority to effect valuable improvement schemes.

### No. 6.—Compulsory Purchase of Land.

In many cases compulsory purchase is absolutely necessary, and it must therefore be shortened, cheapened and simplified. Up to the present the compulsory purchase of land has involved the ratepayers, in many instances, in an unnecessary outlay, and what is suggested is that the compulsory purchase price of land required by public bodies should be the capital value of the land upon the register of the valuation authority. Local and imperial taxes should be levied on the value so declared, and any special tax on land values should be assessed on this basis. The result, in the opinion of many local authorities, would be that cheaper land would come into the market and that large areas suitable for building purposes, which otherwise would have been reserved, would be at the disposal of public bodies.

### No. 7.—Rapid Transit.

Owing to the immense size of the modern town, the whole question of town development will turn on rapid transit, and the electric tram is perhaps the most potent force in determining what will be the lines upon which the town will develop. London, of course, is exceptional, and nothing but the appointment of a Traffic Board, as recommended by the Commission, will meet the whole difficulty. But for the average large town so far as the housing question concerns the working classes, what is required is the possibility of quick electric traction from the centre to the circumference. The town will grow wherever this is possible, and in order to ensure the proper development of the town, the trams should be in the hands of the local authorities. If this were the case, the purchase of land by the local authority along the main roads would insure lower rents as the town developed, and in the end as a result in the increase of value, lower rates.

## No. 8.—Revision of Bye-Laws.

There is considerable need for the revision of
bye-laws especially in the town.    The Select
Committee points out that in the country, where
there are no bye-laws, there has still been comparatively little done to meet the demand for
labourers' cottages.    In the town, however, what
is required is a strengthening of the bye-laws in
the direction of securing more open spaces and
larger gardens where new housing estates are
developed.    If this were accomplished we might
have Bournvilles surrounding our great cities
instead of the hideous congeries of suburban slums
which can be seen in some parts of greater London.
The number of houses or rooms to the acre should
be strictly limited, and in that way it might be
possible to limit the number of inhabitants to the
acre.    By drawing a distinction between streets of
comparative unimportance and main roads, and
enabling the former to be constructed more
cheaply, our main roads might be largely improved,
while the rents of cottages in the side streets
might be appreciably lessened.    Within certain
limits experiments in the use of new materials and
new methods of construction should be encouraged by the local authority.

These are some of the main points which call
for attention, and although it might be found after
a time that considerable alteration in detail was
required, yet it is upon some such lines that the
housing problem will be solved, as solved it must

be if, both from the point of view of physique and morality, we are to keep our position in the forefront of the nations. " The home-loving peoples have been the strong peoples in all times." It is the duty of the State and of the local authority to make possible that love of home, without which our national life must inevitably deteriorate.

L

# APPENDIX NO. I

## NATIONAL HOUSING REFORM COUNCIL.

### MEMORANDUM ON PRACTICAL POINTS OF HOUSING REFORM.

#### I.—Survey of Housing Conditions, etc.

*(Section 92 of Public Health Act, 1875, and Section 32 of the Housing of the Working Classes Act.)*

The above Sections should be so amended as to secure :—

(a) Compulsory house-to-house inspection in every street of every district, instead of the intermittent or partial inspection now generally made.

(b) That a complete report and summary of such survey results in each district should be sent to the Central Authority with the Medical Officer of Health's report; that these reports should be classified according to rates of mortality and disease, and that special public enquiries should be systematically held locally by the Central Authority in regard to the worst cases.

(c) That a definite power of entry for the purpose of inspection should be given to the officers of the Sanitary Authority.

154

(*d*) That a register or record of all houses should be kept and reviewed at least quinquennially, showing in respect of every dwelling the size, number and rent of rooms, light and air space, sanitary condition and state of repair, and the names and addresses of the owner or owners of sites and buildings.

(*e*) That Government Health and Housing Inspectors should be appointed to report to the Central Authority concerning the action or otherwise of Local Authorities in regard to the health and housing duties placed upon them under the Public Health and Housing Acts.

## II.—Repair or Closing of Dilapidated or Unhealthy Dwellings.

(*Sections* 91 *to* 96, *Public Health Act, and Sections* 30 *to* 39 *of Part II. Housing of the Working Classes Act,* 1890.)

These Sections should be so amended as to secure :—

(*a*) That houses in a bad state of repair or neglected as regards whitewashing, painting, papering, etc., should be included in the definition of " nuisances " (Sec. 91) and dealt with accordingly under the other sections, so as to compel owners and occupiers to keep their houses structurally sound, safe, presentable, and cleanly.

> (At present these sections are confined to sanitary defects that can be proved " dangerous or injurious to health.")

(*b*) The procedure in regard to Closing Orders should be amended so as to enable a Local Authority, if a house is proved to be unfit for human habitation, to itself make a Provisional Order which shall take effect, unless an appeal be made within fourteen days to the local Magistrates, in which case it should be for the latter to either finally confirm or to disallow it.

(*c*) When a Closing Order has been made, but not before, the Local Authority should be obliged to give a specification of repairs required, to render the premises fit for human habitation in accordance with the definition laid down in, and these repairs should be executed to the satisfaction of the Local Authority before the Closing Order is rescinded. Any dispute in regard to this between the owner and the Local Authority to be settled by the Local Government Board.

(*d*) Demolition of insanitary houses should automatically follow the Closing Order if the repairs are not satisfactorily executed within twelve months of the issue of the Closing Order, without it being necessary for the Local Authority to prove that the houses are dangerous or injurious to the health of the neighbourhood.

(*e*) If the Local Authority can prove that any houses forming a group or part of a group of ten or twelve houses have not sufficient air space, then the Magistrates *shall* order a sufficient number of them to be removed as Obstructive Buildings to provide the minimum of air space for each house. This minimum to be not less than 50 per cent. of the open space required under the model Bye-Laws.

(*f*) The process of arbitration for settling the amount of compensation to be paid by the Local Authority for Obstructive Buildings to be simplified.

## III.—Overcrowding.

### (*Public Health Act*, 1875.)

(*a*) A minimum standard of 500 cubic feet per adult should be fixed as to air space where a room is used by day and slept in by night, and 400 cubic feet where the room is only slept in.

(*b*) The notice to abate overcrowding should be served on the owner, who should be liable to increasing penalties for permitting more than the number of persons prescribed in a clear definition of overcrowding laid down by the amended Act.

(c) Scheduled streets or groups of houses should be subject to the powers as possessed by the Glasgow Council, which enable them to ticket one and two room tenements.

## IV.—Acquisition of Land.

*Sections 175 to 178, Public Health Act, 1875; Section 57, Housing Act, 1890; Section 7, Housing Act, 1900.)*

The sections of the principal Acts dealing with the acquisition and holding of land should be amended by adding to, or where necessary substituting for, the provisions of the Lands Clauses Acts, the following powers :—

(a) That Local Authorities (subject, in the case of Parish and District Councils, to the consent of the higher authorities) should be allowed to buy land in large quantities to use, or hold, or lease, without necessarily specifying any definite immediate purpose or detailed scheme.

(b) That the basis of any compulsory purchase of land required by public bodies should be the capital value of the land as declared by the proper Valuation Authority, or by Special Commissioners, as in the case of the Income Tax (subject to an additional exceptional allowance of a predetermined and limited extra precentage for Severance and other special circumstances) ; and that on the value so declared local and imperial taxes on land shall be levied (except where otherwise expressly excluded), and in particular that any special tax on land values hereafter imposed shall be so assessed.

*(See also Bill 102, and Clauses 3 and 5 of Bill 104.)*

## V.—Town Extension and Development.

(a) A Central Board of Commissioners to deal with Land, Housing and Transit questions should be appointed to consider the main conditions of growth of the various districts in the country, and to act in the first place as a kind of Boundary Commission to plan out what may be called "Scientific Areas," for each of which there shall be subsequently established a Statutory Committee consisting as to a majority of two-thirds of representatives of Local Authorities, and as to the remainder experts nominated by the Central Board of Commissioners.

(b) The Central Commissioners and the Statutory Committee should be empowered to buy up or help local Councils to buy from time to time large belts of land. They should be empowered to raise loans and issue, if desirable, guaranteed land stock to enable them to buy land or help other public bodies to do so.

(c) The District Committee should be empowered to make or request local councils to make plans for Town extension, dealing specially with the development of the belts of land surrounding towns and prepared in good time so as to meet future needs (somewhat on the lines adopted in many German towns and combined districts), and to create separate districts for residential and manufacturing purposes with different building regulations.

### VI.—Cheaper Money.

(*Sections* 65 *to* 69, *Housing Working Classes Act*, 1890 ; *Sections* 233 *to* 244, *Public Health Act*, 1875 ; *Public Works Loans Acts* 1875 *and* 1897.)

The above sections should be amended so as to provide for :—

(a) The lending of money by the Public Works Loans Commissioners to public bodies or societies of public utility, specially recognised as such by the Central Authority, at the lowest market rate at which the Government can raise money, plus an allowance of $\frac{1}{8}$ of one per cent. if necessary for management expenses.

(*b*) To societies of public utility, specially recognised as such by the Central Authority, loans under Section 67 of the Act of 1890 to be increased from the present maximum of 50 per cent. to an amount not exceeding 75 per cent.

> NOTE.—It has been suggested that a portion of the Savings Bank Funds might be utilized for special Housing Loans. This has been already done with success in Belgium.

(*d*) Municipalities to be empowered to provide land and make roads and sewers, and to lend money to such societies of public utility in exchange for definite measures of control and advantageous conditions as to rents, air space, and other matters beneficial to the tenants and the community generally.

### VII.—Cheaper Building.

> (*Sections* 157 *to* 159, *Public Health Act*, 1875 ; *Part III.,
> Public Health Act*, 1890.)

(*a*) The Building Bye-laws should be revised, especially as regards the construction of small streets and the structure of walls and buildings.

(*b*) Four ratepayers should be empowered to require any local authority to consider necessary revisions of their bye-laws in the light of improvements and modifications of the model bye-laws made from time to time, especially in regard to the better planning of streets, etc.

(*c*) Bye-laws should be strengthened in the direction of securing that more land should be attached to dwellings when any new housing estate is developed. There should be a Clause prohibiting, except under special conditions, the building of more than a certain number of rooms—say 100 —per acre.

> NOTE.—The limiting of the number of rooms per acre will meet the case of both cottage districts in England and tenement districts in Scotland.

### VIII.—Organisation.

(a) Any four householders or electors should have the power to make a representation where the supply of dwellings is inadequate or inferior in quality, and to require the local authority to provide or promote the provision of new dwellings if the representation be substantiated.

(b) Committees on the lines of the Comités de Patronage in Belgium and France (for stimulating public interest); and such Societies as the Sociétés de Crédit and the Sociétés de Construction should be encouraged and promoted by national and local assistance from public bodies.

(c) The utilisation of the land acquired as suggested in IV. should, subject to the consent of the Local Authority, be thrown open on suitable leasehold conditions to all agencies willing to accept proper conditions as the provision of suitable dwellings at reasonable rents, with proper air space and other matters beneficial to the tenants and the community generally.

### IX.—General.

*(Section 53, Act of 1890.)*

That the Local Authority should be empowered to provide a garden of three acres or even more, with cottages erected under Part III. of the Housing Act.

*(Sections 149 to 156, Public Health Act, 1875.)*

Powers should be conferred for preventing the disfigurement of beautiful streets or districts.

# APPENDIX NO. II.

## THE LOCAL GOVERNMENT BOARD FOR IRELAND.

### THE LABOURERS (IRELAND) ORDER, 1906.

In pursuance of the powers vested by the Labourers (Ireland) Acts 1883–1906 in the Local Government Board for Ireland, the Board has issued rules and regulations under the said Acts, of which the following are four Clauses : —

4. A representation for the purposes of the Acts may be made in one of the Forms numbered 1 to 7 inclusive.

5. Every Council shall provide and keep at all times available a supply of forms of representation and shall give a form free of charge to any ratepayer or labourer applying for the same.

6. Within one month from the first day of November, 1906, every Council shall give public notice by means of advertisements (Form 37) in some two or more newspapers circulating in the district, and placards posted throughout the district, that representations for the purposes of the Acts may be lodged with their Clerk on any day up to the first day of February, 1907.

7. All representations lodged as aforesaid shall be submitted to the Council at their meeting next following the first day of February, 1907, and the Council shall thereupon fix a date, not later than fourteen days thereafter, upon which a meeting of the Council shall be held for the consideration of the representation.

The most important forms of representation are as follows : —

(Additional Cottages to be provided).

........................Rural District.

........................District Electoral Division.

We, the undersigned, being agricultural labourers or ratepayers, represent that there is not a sufficient number of houses available for the accommodation of agricultural labourers in the above-named Electoral Division, and that it is the duty of the District Council to take proceedings under the Labourers Act for the making of an improvement scheme in respect of such Electoral Division.

We suggest that cottages should be built with suitable plots of land attached thereon on the holdings, and for the agricultural labourers mentioned in the Schedule given below.

*(Then follow signatures and addresses together with schedule of particulars).*

Form 2.

## LABOURERS (IRELAND) ACTS 1883 TO 1906.

***

(Cottages to be built in substitution for insanitary dwellings).

........................Rural District.

........................District Electoral Division.

We, the undersigned, being agricultural labourers or ratepayers, represent that the undermentioned labourers are living in houses which are unfit for human habitation and should be provided with suitable house accommodation, and that it is the duty of the District Council to take proceedings under the Labourers Acts for the making of an improvement scheme in respect of the above-named Electoral Division.

We suggest that cottages should be built in lieu of these dwellings on the holdings named in the Schedule set out below, and that suitable plots or gardens should be attached thereto.

Form 5.

## LABOURERS (IRELAND) ACTS 1883 TO 1906.

### REPRESENTATION.

(Houses to be acquired and repaired.)

........................Rural District.

........................District Electoral Division.

We, the undersigned, being agricultural labourers or ratepayers, represent that the houses mentioned in the Schedule attached hereto are in need of improvements and repairs to render them suitable as labourers' cottages, and that it is the dnty of the District Council to take proceedings under the Labourers Acts for the making of an improvement scheme in respect of such Electoral Division.

We suggest that these houses should be acquired by the Council, improved and repaired, and that suitable plots of land should be acquired in conjunction therewith.

Form 6.

## LABOURERS (IRELAND) ACTS 1883 TO 1906.

### REPRESENTATION.

———

(Tracts of land to be acquired.)

.............................Rural District.

.........................District Electoral Division.

We, the undersigned, being agricultural labourers or ratepayers, represent to the Rural District Council that a necessity exists for the acquisition of the tract or tracts of land referred to in the Schedule hereto with a view to the same being parcelled out in allotments among the agricultural labourers whose names are set out in the Schedule.

And we do further represent that it is the duty of the District Council to take proceedings under the Labourers Acts for the making of an improvement scheme in respect of such Electoral Division.

# BIBLIOGRAPHY.

Royal Commission on the Housing of the Working Classes (1885).

Special Report on the Housing of the Working Classes Amendment Act (1906).

Report by Medical Officer of Health on the Floodgate Street Area in Birmingham. (Housing Committee, Birmingham).

Glasgow Municipal Commission on the Housing of the Poor. Wm. Hodge & Co.

"Extracts from Minutes of Evidence. . . . Municipal Commission on the Housing of the Poor. . . . Glasgow, 1903." (Also Appendix to Report of Housing Committee, October 20th, 1903). Percival Jones, Ltd., Town Hall Printing Works, Edward Street, Birmingham. 1904.

"The Dwellings of the Poor." Reports of the Mansion House Council, 1884-1906. (1s. each). 31 Imperial Buildings, Ludgate Circus.

Report of Proceedings at Conference as to Cheap Dwellings. 1901. Glasgow. Robert Anderson, Glasgow.

"Leeds' Slumdom." D. B. Foster. C. H. Halliday, Leeds. 6d. net. (1896).

National Conference on Housing. Westminster Palace Hotel (1901). Land Law Reform Association. 1d.

165

REPORT OF THE TENEMENT HOUSE COMMISSION, NEW YORK. 2 vols. (1903).

ANTI-BUILDING BY-LAWS. Suggestions for Reform. R. M. Lucas. (Mate & Sons, Southampton. 1s.)

REPORT OF THE COMMITTEE ON THE HOUSING OF THE POOR (1902). Manchester Diocesan Conference. (John Heywood, Manchester. 2d.)

"HOUSING IMPROVEMENT." F. M. Lupton (1906). A Summary of Ten Years' Work in Leeds. Jowett & Sowry, Leeds.

"HOUSING CONDITIONS IN MANCHESTER AND SALFORD. Sherratt & Hughes. T. R. Marr (1904). 1s.

"REPORT OF THE HOUSING COMMITTEE, BIRMINGHAM." Percival Jones, Birmingham. 2s. 6d. (1906).

"THE HOUSING OF THE WORKING CLASSES, BATH." Harding & Co., Bath (1901).

"THE HOUSING QUESTION IN CROYDON." H. T. Muggeridge. The Croydon Housing Committee (1901). 1d.

"NO ROOM TO LIVE IN GUILDFORD." Y.M.C.A., Guildford (1902).

"RESULTS OF HOUSE-TO-HOUSE INQUIRY IN CLARENDON STREET AREA." Housing Committee, Paddington (1901).

"REPORT OF INTERNATIONAL CONGRESS ON THE HOUSING OF THE WORKING CLASSES HELD AT PARIS IN JUNE, 1900. P. S. King & Son. 1s.

"PROBLEMS OF A SCOTTISH PROVINCIAL TOWN (Dunfermline). T. H. Whitehouse. George Allen (1905). 3s. 6d. net.

"THE HOUSING PROBLEM IN THE TOWN." C. M. Knowles. "Eighty" Club Pamphlet (out of print).

"A HOUSING POLICY." John S. Nettlefold. Cornish Bros., Birmingham (1905).

"THE HOUSING HANDBOOK." W. Thompson (1903). P. S. King & Son. 2s. 6d. net.

"HOMES OF THE LONDON POOR." Octavia Hill (1883). Macmillan. 1s. net.

"PUBLIC HEALTH AND HOUSING." John F. J. Sykes, M.D. (1901). P. S. King & Son. 3s. 6d.

"DWELLINGS OF THE PEOPLE." T. Locke Worthington (1901). Swan Sonnenschein. 2s. 6d.

"THE EXAMPLE OF GERMANY." T. C. Horsfall (1905). University Press, Manchester. 1s. net.

"THE HOUSING OF THE WORKING CLASSES." Edward Bowmaker, M.D. (1895). Methuen & Co. 2s. 6d.

"HOUSING IN TOWN AND COUNTRY." Papers and Addresses (1906). Garden City Press. 6d.

"THE HOUSING QUESTION IN LONDON." (1855 to 1900). C. J. Stewart for London County Council. P. S. King & Son.

"THE HOUSING QUESTION." Alfred Smith, L.C.C. Swan Sonnenschein. 1s. net.

"THE ENGLISHMAN'S CASTLE." George Haw. C. W. Daniel, 3, Amen Corner (1906). 3d.

"HOUSING BY VOLUNTARY ENTERPRISE." James Parsons. P. S. King & Son (1903). 2s. 6d. net.

"MODERN HOUSING IN TOWN AND COUNTRY." James Cornes. Batsford, 94, High Holborn (1905). 7s. 6d.

"POVERTY." B. Seebohm Rowntree. Macmillan (1903). 1s.

"FABIAN TRACT." No. 101. Fabian Society (1901). 1d. Also Tracts 63, 76 and 103.

"SOME EXPERIMENTS IN HOUSING." (1891-1901). Glasgow Workmen's Dwelling Co. 1s.

"LIFE AND LABOUR IN LONDON." Charles Booth. Final Vol. Macmillan (1902). 5s.

"REPORT ON THE PUBLIC HEALTH OF FINSBURY." 1905 and 1906. George Newman, M.D. Bean & Son.

"NO ROOM TO LIVE." George Haw. 2s. 6d. Clarion Press.

"BRITAIN'S HOMES." George Haw. 2s. 6d. Clarion Press.

"THE HOUSING PROBLEM AND THE MUNICIPALITY." W. Smart, LL.D. 1d. Adshead (1902). Glasgow.

"LIFE IN WEST LONDON." A. Sherwell. Methuen & Co. (1901). 2s. 6d.

"THE LONDON PROGRAMME." Sidney Webb. Swan Sonnenschein (1891). 1s.

"Housing the People, an Example in Co-operation."
Sir Hugh Gilzean-Reid. Alexander Gardner,
Paternoster Square (1895). 1s.

"Better Homes for Workers and How to obtain
them." H. R. Aldridge, Land Nationalisation
Society (1901). 1d.

"The Improvement of Towns and Cities." C. M.
Robinson. Putnam (1901). 5s.

"Modern Civic Art, The City made Beautiful."
C. M. Robinson. Putnam (1903). 10s. 6d.

"Rural England." Rider Haggard. 2 Vols. 21s.
Longmans (1906).

"Land Reform." Right Hon. Jesse Collings. Longmans (1906). 12s. 6d.

"Garden Cities in Theory and Practice." A. R.
Sennett. 2 Vols. Bemrose (1905). 21s.

"Country Cottages," by "Home Counties" (1905).
Wm. Heineman. 6s. net.

"The Cottage Homes of England." W. Walter
Crotch (1901). P. S. King & Son. 2s. net.

"The Rural Exodus." P. Anderson Graham.
Methuen & Co. (1892). 2s. 6d.

"The Labourer and his Cottage." Robert Williams
and Fred Knee. Twentieth Century Press (1905).
3s. net.

"Cheap Dwellings." Paul N. Hasluck (1905).
Cassell & Co. 1s. net.

"Bad Housing in Rural Districts." Clement
Edwards. Paper in Fabian Tract, 101.

"Labourers' Cottages." Miss Constance Cochrane.
Papers i. and ii. in Fabian Tract, 101.

"The Garden City Movement." C. Montagu Harris,
M.A. Garden City Press (1905). 6d. net.

"Garden Suburbs, Villages and Homes." Garden
City Press (1906). 6d. net.

The Book of the Cheap Cottages Exhibition." The
Country Gentleman and Land and Water," Ltd.,
Dean Street, Holborn (1905). 1s.

"Garden Cities of To-morrow." Ebenezer Howard. Swan Sonnenschein. (1902). 1s. 6d.

"Garden Suburbs." Chas. Howes, 38, Baldwin Street, Bristol. (1902). 1d.

"The Garden City and Agriculture." Thos. Adams. Garden City Press. (1905). 1s.

"The Carnegie Dunfermline Trust." Clark & Son, Dunfermline. (1903).

## RAPID TRANSIT.

"The Transit Problem in Cities." Jn. P. Fox. *World's Work and Play*, September, 1906.

"Railways and their Rates." Edwin A. Pratt. John Murray. (1906). 1s.

"Modern City Traffic." *Municipal Journal*, October 12th and October 19th, 1906. Lynden Macassey, M.A. (Secretary to Royal Commission).

Report of the Royal Commission on the Means of Locomotion and Transport in London. (1905). Wyman & Sons. Vols. I.—VIII. (Vol. I. contains the Recommendation of the Commission).

## TAXATION OF LAND VALUES.

"The Rating of Land Values." A. Wilson Fox, C.B. P. S. King. (1906). 3s. 6d. Net.

"Coming Men on Coming Questions." No. XX. Edited by W. T. Stead. Chas. Trevelyan, M.P.

"The Taxation of Land Values." Reprinted from *Westminster Review*. By Baillie Ferguson.

Pamphlets of "English League for Taxation of Land Values."

Report on Land Legislation in Australasia. (5d.) c. 3191.

"Local Taxation in London." M. E. Lange. King & Son. (1906). 1s.

"Land Values." Josiah C. Wedgwood M.P. Garden City Press. 3s. (1907).

M

# LIST OF HOUSING, SANITARY, LAND AND REFORM ASSOCIATIONS.

Manchester and Salford Citizens' Association for the Improvement of the Homes and Surroundings of the People. Ancoats Museum.

Sheffield Association for Promoting Sanitary Reform and the Better Housing of the Poor. Office, 16, St. James' Street, Sheffield.

Nottingham and District Housing Committee, 11, Houseman Street, Nottingham.

York Health and Housing Reform Association, 63, Gillygate, York.

Cheshunt Workmen's Housing League.

Seaham Harbour Housing Reform Council, 12, Vane Terrace, Seaham Harbour.

Three Towns' Housing Association—Plymouth, Devonport and Stonehouse, 23, Gifford Street, Plymouth.

Birmingham Trades' Council Housing Committee.

Leeds Sanitary Aid Society. The Rev. Edgar Gibson, D.D., Vicar of Leeds, Chairman.

Derby and District Housing Reform Association, 91, Stockbrook Street, Derby.

Liverpool Housing Association.

Bristol Committee for Promoting the Better Housing of the Poor. The Rev. P. A. Phelps, M.A., Chairman, 17, Small Street, Bristol.

Coventry Housing Reform Council, 74, Godiva Street, Coventry.

Newcastle and Gateshead Housing Reform Council, 53, Cavendish Road, Jesmond, Newcastle.

Dundee and District Housing Reform Council, 12, Blyth Street, Dundee.

National Housing Reform Council. Office, 432, West Strand, London, W.C.

Wakefield and District Sanitary Aid Society. The Bishop of Wakefield, Chairman. Office, King Street Chambers, Wakefield.

Mansion House Council on the Dwellings of the Poor, Imperial Buildings, Ludgate Circus, E.C.

Wolverhampton Housing Committee, 46, Ewen's Street, Wolverhampton.

Sunderland Housing Reform Council, 30, Ridley Terrace, Sunderland.

Durham Land and Labour Committee, Miners' Hall, Durham.

Northumberland Land and Labour Committee, Burt Hall, Newcastle-on-Tyne.

Leicestershire Housing Committee, 59, Dulverton Road, Leicester.

Bristol Garden Suburbs Association Ltd., 1, Queen Anne's Buildings, Baldwin Street, Bristol.

Christian Social Union, 102, Adelaide Road, N.W.

Friends' Social Union, 1 Woburn Square, W.C.

Wesleyan Union for Social Service, Rev. W. F. Lofthouse, Friary Road, Handsworth, Birmingham.

Peabody Donation Fund, 5, Victoria Street, S.W.

The Guiness Trust, 64, Queen Street, Cheapside.

East End Dwellings Co., Ltd., 27, Chancery Lane, W.C.

The Artisans, Labourers', and General Dwellings Co., Ltd., 16, Great George Street, Westminster.

Rowton Houses, Ltd., 16, Great George Street, Westminster.

Metropolitan Public Gardens Association, 83, Lancaster Gate, W.

Birmingham Rowton House, 37, Newball Street, Birmingham.

The Provident Association of London, Ltd., 72, Bishopsgate Street Without, E.C.

Garden City Tenants, Ltd., 22, Red Lion Square, W.C.

Co-partnership Tenants' Housing Council, 22, Red Lion Square, W.C.

The Ealing Tenants, Ltd., Woodfield Road, Ealing, W.

The Wharncliffe Dwellings Co., Ltd., 16, Great George Street, Westminster.

Social Service (Tenements) Co., Ltd., 34, Trinity College, Dublin.

Metropolitan Association for Improving the Dwellings of the Industrious Classes, 1, Pancras Square, N.W.

Land Law Reform Association, 21, John Street, Adelphi, W.C.

Workmen's National Housing Council, 53A Fetter Lane, E.C.

Garden City Association, 348, Birkbeck Bank Chambers, Holborn, W.C.

The Co-operative Small Holdings Society, 10, Adelphi Terrace, W.C.

Rural Housing and Sanitation Association, 9, Southampton Street, Holborn, W.C.

Land Nationalisation Society, 432, West Strand, W.C.

English League for the Taxation of Land Values, 376, Strand, W.C.

Allotments and Small Holdings Association, 116, Vivian Road, Harborne, Birmingham.

London Reform Union, F. W. Galton, Trafalgar Buildings, Northumberland Avenue, W.C.

Outer London Inquiry, School of Economics, Clare Market, W.C.

East London Tenants' Protection Committee, Toynbee Hall, 28, Commercial Street, E.

British Institute of Social Service, 11, Southampton Row, W.C.

# INDEX.

---

HEADLEY BROTHERS, PRINTERS, LONDON AND ASHFORD.